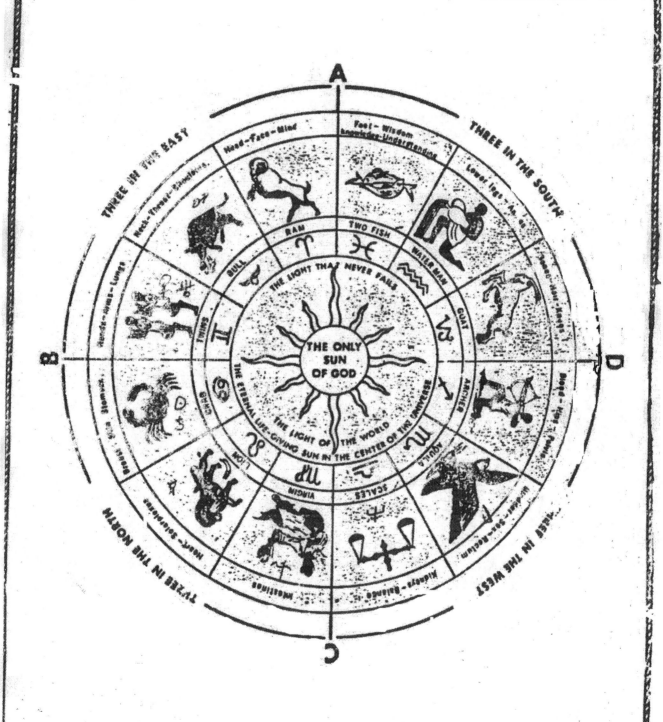

ENTER NATIONALNOMICS (THE KING-DOM OF DIVINE FREE-DOM) THE MOORISH CODE

ENTER NATIONALNOMICS -THE MOORISH ZODIAC CONSTITUTION THE GREAT SEAL...

T. KING CONNALLY-BEY

Order this book online at www.trafford.com
or email orders@trafford.com

Most Trafford titles are also available at major online book retailers.

Printed in the United States of America.

ISBN: 978-1-4669-8185-0 (sc)
ISBN: 978-1-4669-8186-7 (e)

Trafford rev. 02/15/2014

North America & international
toll-free: 1 888 232 4444 (USA & Canada)
fax: 812 355 4082

DEDICATIONS

This Manuscript is Dedicated to our Children Queen, Saladin, King, Amen RA and Mustafa Akeem and All the Children of the World (Especially Shameeka & Son Mikah and Amir as well as Lil Jay (Nunu), Keshawn, Lil. Lay Lay, Jayla, Nana, Lil. Grandma (Teara), Britney, Lil. Bradon, Lil. Tyann Madina, Velvet Song, JaKwan, Jameek, Mandel, Destiny, Lil. Dashawn (Lil Jack), Fred the Wise Head, & Lil Jahar as well as Taleek, Tarik, Coby, Jay, Marques, Sincere, Ms. Edna, Keisha, Nia, Mya, Deatrich, Shamond, Tandra, Naisia, R.J., Tiffany,as well as all Swinney Children and James Children and Grands, and Blessed, Lil. Miakiel, The Twins, Cory, Tory, Lil. Alex, London, A.J. & Alex, Cre and Pre.

With Special Dedications to my SON of YA, who aided my Thinking within, during the course of bringing this together, Markey, Lashawn, Frenchie 1017, Waka Flocka, Elijah, Brianna, Evan and Bro. Bee Daley and all Moorish young "Beys & Els", "Als & Deys, Etc., Etc., Etc . . .

Also dedication goes to All the Elders of the Family and of the World who are striving to Uplift fallen humanity (Especially Mother Love), Heru (Horus) and all the First Born, The GOD NATION, ZOOLU NATION, N.O.I. HEBREW ISRAELITES, CHURCHES OF ALL DENOMINATIONS, MUSLIM WORLD, Min. Farrah Khan & (Father Time)! For One Only Learns what One Teaches Self! Each One, Teach One, In Order to Reach One (Self)! Now Save YOURSELF . . .

Nationality is the Order of the Day (Now Proclaim Your Nationality and Enter-Nationalnomics) {The Kingdom of Divine Freedom}! Kun fi ya kun (Say Be and it shall be)!

ACKNOWLEDGEMENTS

This is Our GIFT to World Development and Our Soul Sacrifice to the Uplifting of fallen humanity!

We give Honors to Clerance 13 X, aka The Father Allah for Revealing and Bringing Us the Light;

We give Honors to Noble Drew Ali, aka Our Prophet for Revealing and Expanding Our Light;

We give Honors to Charles Mosley-Bey, aka The Supreme Master for Revealing and Shining our Light;

We give Honors to All Grand Sheiks and Governor Heads of the M.S.T. of A for Revealing and Spreading Our Light;

We give Honors to All Moorish Officials, Members and Moorish Movements for Revealing and Being the Light;

We give Honors to Marcus Moziah Garvey, aka The Forerunner for Revealing and Preparing our Light;

We give Honors to Muhammad (PBUH), aka The Prophet for Revealing and Confirming Our Light;

We give Honors to All the Asiatic Scholars of Egyptology aka Master Minds for Revealing and Directing Our Light;

We give a Special and High Honors to Bro. Yon-t and All New Comers & Members for Having and Receiving the Light;

We give Honors to Bro. Reginald Lewis of Beatrice International, aka "The First That Ever Did It" for his financial guidance and acquisition enlightenment of the Business World;

We give Honors to Mr. Warren Buffet, aka the Financial Market Guru, for many years of patience and continued Financial Enlightenment;

We give Honors to Mr. Jack Welsh, aka the King of CEO'S in the Business World, for keeping me on point and very well focused;

We give High Honors to All Our Spiritual Teachers and Spiritual Advisors for continued guidance and Conscious Enlightenment;

We give Honors to Nelson Mandela, aka The Father Teacher of Tolerance and Patience of All Nations of the World and Winnie;

We give Honors to President Obama, aka 'The Chosen' for the Divine Work he was called to Do;

We give Honors to All Our Family Members, Our Siblings, especially our Sister Princess (Dr. Teara Connally Fields) Who is always striving to make the world a better place, Founder of (Women of Extreme Vision):

We give Honors to All Our Business Associates & Companions throughout the World for their Moral Support:

Last, but not least, We give Special Honors to Our Parents, aka Popa Joop and Queen Mumu (Bob & Gwen) for allowing us to come through them to complete the Divine Work (Assignment) We were called to pursue and finally Do.

TABLE OF CONTENTS

It takes a Large Book to hide the Truth, it takes a small book to reveal the Truth.
moorishperpetualunion@aol.com

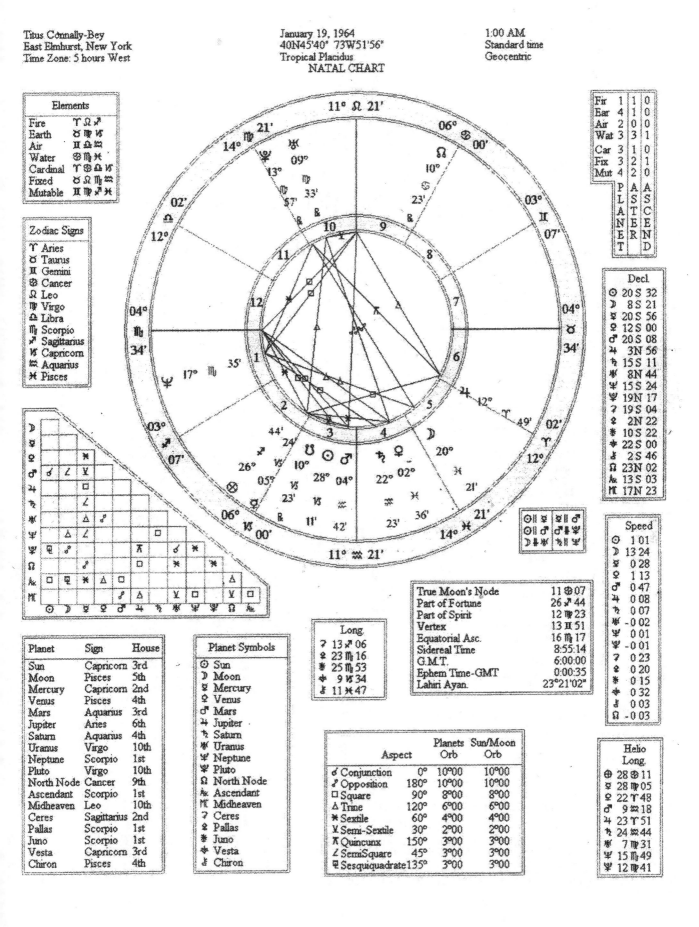

Titus Connally-Bey East Elmhurst, New York Time Zone: 5 hours West	January 19, 1964 40N45'40" 73W51'56" Tropical Placidus	1:00 AM Standard time Geocentric

NATAL CHART

Elements	
Fire	♈ ♌ ♐
Earth	♉ ♍ ♑
Air	♊ ♎ ♒
Water	♋ ♏ ♓
Cardinal	♈ ♋ ♎ ♑
Fixed	♉ ♌ ♏ ♒
Mutable	♊ ♍ ♐ ♓

	PLANET	ASTER	ASCEND
Fir	1	1	0
Ear	4	1	0
Air	2	0	0
Wat	3	3	1
Car	3	1	0
Fix	3	2	1
Mut	4	2	0

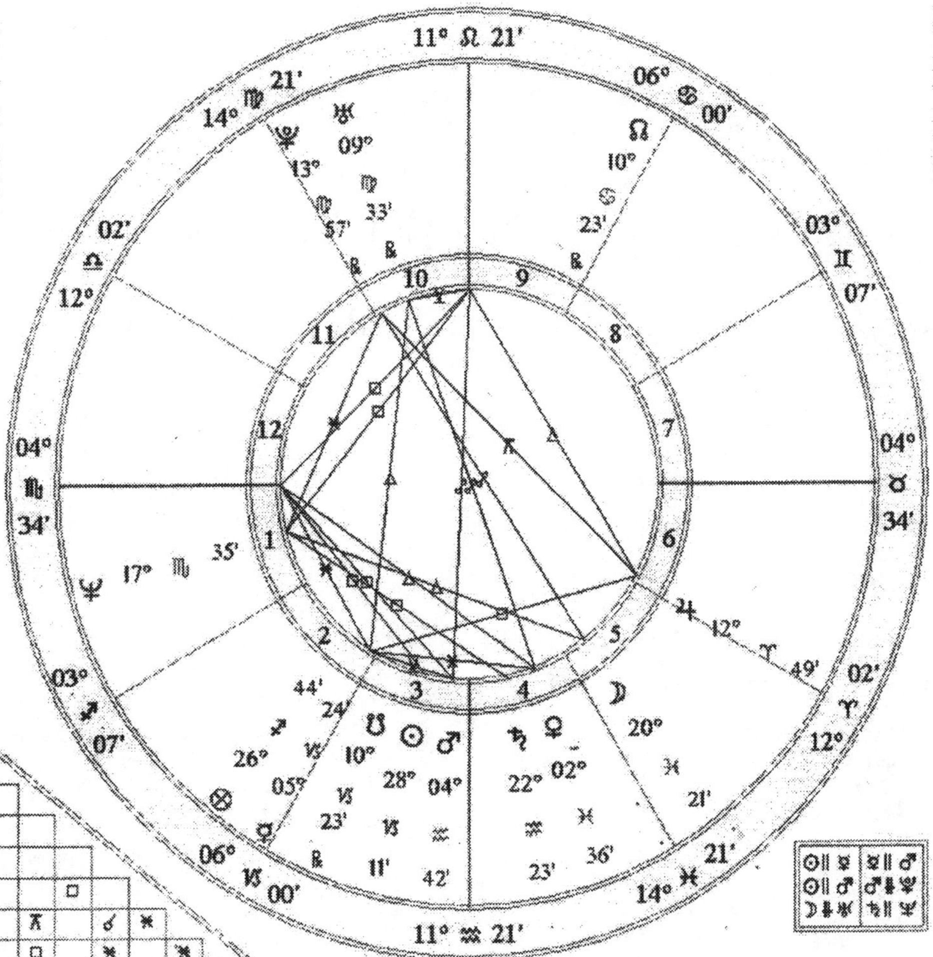

Zodiac Signs
♈ Aries
♉ Taurus
♊ Gemini
♋ Cancer
♌ Leo
♍ Virgo
♎ Libra
♏ Scorpio
♐ Sagittarius
♑ Capricorn
♒ Aquarius
♓ Pisces

Decl.	
☉	20 S 32
☽	8 S 21
☿	20 S 56
♀	12 S 00
♂	20 S 08
♃	3N 56
♄	15 S 11
♅	8N 44
♆	15 S 24
♇	19N 17
⚳	19 S 04
⚴	2N 22
⚵	10 S 22
⚶	22 S 00
⚷	2 S 46
☊	23N 02
As	13 S 03
MC	17N 23

	☉	☽	☿	♀	♂	♃	♄	♅	♆	♇	☊	As
☽												
☿												
♀			⚹									
♂	☌	∠	⚺									
♃			□									
♄			∠									
♅			△	☍								
♆		△	∠				□					
♇	⚼	☍				⚻		☌	⚹			
☊			☍			□		⚹		⚹		
As	□	⚼	⚹	△	□						△	
MC					☍	△		⚺	□		⚺	□

☉ ∥ ☿	☿ ∥ ♂
☉ ∥ ♂	♂ ⋕ ♇
☽ ⋕ ♅	♄ ∥ ♆

Speed	
☉	1 01
☽	13 24
☿	0 28
♀	1 13
♂	0 47
♃	0 08
♄	0 07
♅	-0 02
♆	0 01
♇	-0 01
⚳	0 23
⚴	0 20
⚵	0 15
⚶	0 32
⚷	0 03
☊	-0 03

True Moon's Node	11 ♋ 07
Part of Fortune	26 ♐ 44
Part of Spirit	12 ♍ 23
Vertex	13 ♊ 51
Equatorial Asc.	16 ♏ 17
Sidereal Time	8:55:14
G.M.T.	6:00:00
Ephem Time-GMT	0:00:35
Lahiri Ayan.	23°21'02"

Long.	
⚳	13 ♐ 06
⚴	23 ♏ 16
⚵	25 ♏ 53
⚶	9 ♑ 34
⚷	11 ♓ 47

Planet	Sign	House
Sun	Capricorn	3rd
Moon	Pisces	5th
Mercury	Capricorn	2nd
Venus	Pisces	4th
Mars	Aquarius	3rd
Jupiter	Aries	6th
Saturn	Aquarius	4th
Uranus	Virgo	10th
Neptune	Scorpio	1st
Pluto	Virgo	10th
North Node	Cancer	9th
Ascendant	Scorpio	1st
Midheaven	Leo	10th
Ceres	Sagittarius	2nd
Pallas	Scorpio	1st
Juno	Scorpio	1st
Vesta	Capricorn	3rd
Chiron	Pisces	4th

Planet Symbols
☉ Sun
☽ Moon
☿ Mercury
♀ Venus
♂ Mars
♃ Jupiter
♄ Saturn
♅ Uranus
♆ Neptune
♇ Pluto
☊ North Node
As Ascendant
MC Midheaven
⚳ Ceres
⚴ Pallas
⚵ Juno
⚶ Vesta
⚷ Chiron

Aspect		Planets Orb	Sun/Moon Orb
☌ Conjunction	0°	10°00	10°00
☍ Opposition	180°	10°00	10°00
□ Square	90°	8°00	8°00
△ Trine	120°	6°00	6°00
⚹ Sextile	60°	4°00	4°00
⚺ Semi-Sextile	30°	2°00	2°00
⚻ Quincunx	150°	3°00	3°00
∠ SemiSquare	45°	3°00	3°00
⚼ Sesquiquadrate	135°	3°00	3°00

Helio Long.	
⊕	28 ♋ 11
☿	28 ♍ 05
♀	22 ♈ 48
♂	9 ♒ 18
♃	23 ♈ 51
♄	24 ♒ 44
♅	7 ♍ 31
♆	15 ♏ 49
♇	12 ♍ 41

Salvation

 Our God

 Unity

The Moorish Science Temple
OF AMERICA
The Divine Constitution and By-Laws

NOBLE DREW ALI
Founder

ACT 1.—The Grand Sheik and the chairman of the Moorish Science Temple of America is in power to make law and enforce laws with the assistance of the Prophet and the Grand Body of the Moorish Science Temple of America. The assistant Grand Sheik is to assist the Grand Sheik in all affairs if he lives according to Love, Truth, Peace, Freedom and Justice, and it is known before the members of the Moorish Science Temple of America.

ACT 2.—All meetings are to be opened and closed promptly according to the circle seven and Love, Truth, Peace, Freedom and Justice. Friday is our Holy Day of rest, because on a Friday the first man was formed in flesh and on a Friday the first man departed out of flesh and ascended unto his father God Allah, for that cause Friday is the Holy Day for all Moslems all over the world.

ACT 3.—Love, Truth, Peace, Freedom and Justice must be proclaimed and practised by all members of the Moorish Science Temple of America. No member is to put in danger or accuse falsely his brother or sister on any occasion at all that may harm his brother or sister, because Allah is Love.

ACT 4.—All members must preserve these Holy and Divine laws, and all members must obey the laws of the government, because by being a Moorish American, you are a part and partial of the government, and must live the life accordingly.

ACT 5.—This organization of the Moorish Science Temple of America is not to cause any confusion or to overthrow the laws and constitution of the said government but to obey hereby.

ACT 6.—With us all members must proclaim their nationality and we are teaching our people their nationality and their Divine Creed that they may know that they are a part and a partial of this said government, and know that they are not Negroes, Colored Folks, Black People or Ethiopians, because these names were given to slaves by slave holders in 1779 and lasted until 1865 during the time of slavery, but this is a new era of time now, and all men now must proclaim their free national name to be recognized by the government in which they live and the nations of the earth, this is the reason why Allah the Great God of the universe ordained Noble Drew Ali, the Prophet to redeem his people from their sinful ways. The Moorish Americans are the descendants of the ancient Moabites whom inhabited the North Western and South Western shores of Africa.

ACT 7.—All members must promptly attend their meetings and become a part and a partial of all uplifting acts of the Moorish Science Temple of America. Members must pay their dues and keep in line with all necessities of the Moorish Science Temple of America, then you are entitled to the name of, "Faithful". Husband, you must support your wife and children; wife you must obey your husband and take care of your children and look after the duties of your household. Sons and daughters must obey father and mother and be industrious and become a part of the uplifting of fallen humanity. All Moorish Americans must keep their hearts and minds pure with love, and their bodies clean with water. This Divine Covenant is from your Holy Prophet Noble Drew Ali, thru the guidance of his Father God Allah.

MOORISH AMERICAN PRAYER
Allah the Father of the universe, the Father of Love, Truth, Peace, Freedom and Justice. Allah is my protector, my guide and my salvation by night and by day thru his Holy Prophet Drew Ali. "Amen."

THE MOORISH SCIENCE TEMPLE OF AMERICA

Home Office: 48 Inches Street   Mt. Clemens, Michigan

Questionnaire and Additional Laws for
The Moorish Americans
(BY THE PROPHET NOBLE DREW ALI)

ACT 1.—Grand Shieks, and Governors and heads of all Temples, all Businesses; Each said Temple must be approved by the Prophet Noble Drew Ali. Before acting upon by any members, let it be finance property or any line of life that will cause the members to sacrifice finance, etc., that will cause the support of any group of members. Any former officer that violates these laws is subject to be removed from his office under heavy restriction, etc., by the Prophet or the Grand Shiek.

ACT 2.—All members are to attend their adept meetings and their public meetings promptly. If a member is found standing around on their meeting period, shall be fined 50¢ on the first case, and on the second, he will be fined one dollar ($1.00), which will go on your emergency fund. If member is working his monthly dues must be paid, and if he has money in the bank he must subscribe for as much as he is able, to the Moorish Uplifting Fund, because it takes finance to uplift a Nation.

ACT 3.—It is lawful and devine duty of every good member if he is able in finance, to aid me in saving the nation and if he does not, he is an enemy to the cause of uplifting his own people and Justice must catch you. Let it be he or she according to Love, Truth, Peace, Freedom and Justice as I have the power invested in my hands and I will have to enforce the law in order to save the nation.

ACT 4.—All members while making a public speech must not use any assertion against the American flag or speak radical against the church or any member of any organized group, because we are to teach Love, Truth, Peace, Freedom and Justice.

ACT 5.—All members must promptly attend their meetings and send their children to Sunday School, and the teacher must confirm himself to the questionary. And let every member exercise his five senses who is able to do so, because out from your Sunday School comes the guiders of the Nation.

ACT 6.—With us all members must proclaim their nationality and we are teaching our people their nationality and their Divine Creed that they may know that they are a part and partial of this said government, and know that they are not Negroes, Colored Folks, Black People or Ethiopians, because these names were given to slaves by slave holders in 1779 and lasted until 1865 during the time of slavery, but this is a new era of time now, and all men now must proclaim their free national name to be recognized by the government in which they live and the nations of the earth, this is the reason why Allah the Great God of the universe ordained Noble Drew Ali, the Prophet to redeem his people from their sinful ways. The Moorish Americans are the descendants of the ancient Moabites who inhabited the North Western and South Western shores of Africa.

ACT 7.—All members must promptly attend their meetings and become a part and a partial of all uplifting acts of the Moorish Science Temple. Members must pay their dues and keep in line with all necessities of the Moorish Science Temple, then you are entitled to the name of "Faithful." Husband, you must support your wife and children. Wife, you must obey your husband and take care of your children and look after the duties of your household. Sons and daughters must obey father and mother and be industrious and become part of the uplifting of fallen humanity. All Moorish Americans must keep their hearts and minds pure with love, and their bodies clean with water. This Divine Covenant is from your Holy Prophet Noble Drew Ali, through the guidance of his Father, God Allah.

THE CODE OF THE LAWS

OF THE

UNITED STATES OF AMERICA

OF A GENERAL AND PERMANENT CHARACTER

IN FORCE

JANUARY 3, 1935

1934 EDITION

CONSOLIDATED, CODIFIED, SET FORTH AND PUBLISHED IN 1935
IN THE ONE HUNDRED AND FIFTY NINTH YEAR
OF THE REPUBLIC

[WITH ANCILLARIES AND INDEX]

Note: Treatise and Commentary by Bro. Taj Tarik Bey,
Moors Order Of The Roundtable
FOR INSTRUCTIONAL PURPOSES ONLY

Charles Mosley Bey Ph.D., L.L.D., A 3rd, 33rd, 360 Degree Master Mason, Free Moorish Master Astrologer and Moorish Constitution Law Giver (Isonimi) has copyright certificates Registered in the United States Department of Justice under Truth A1-Library of Congress Copyright Office, which reveal, At law, the conditions of Intercourse between the Indigenous Moors and occupational European Nations, with whom the Moors have Treaties. This affirms the pre-existing Status of the Moors in all matters of Interchange, Commerce and Law with the European side of the Nation. The specific Copyright certificate of note: Clock of Destiny, Moorish American Nationality Card of Identification, with Zodiac Constitution. Has:

REGISTRATION NO: AA222141 CLASS A
THIS NUMBER REFERS TO:
THE CODE OF THE LAWS OF THE UNITED STATES OF AMERICA
OF A GENERAL AND PERMANENT CHARACTER
IN FORCE JANUARY 3, 1935   1934 EDITION
Title 22: Chapter 2: Section 141

TITLE 22:   FOREIGN RELATIONS AND INTERCOURSE PAGE 954
Chapter 2:   Consular Court
Section 141:   Judicial authority generally. To carry into full effect the
Provisions of the treaties of the United States with certain foreign countries.

THERE ARE NO STRANGE HAPPENINGS
LAW GOVERNS ALL EVENTS

THE CHRONICLES OF FINANCIAL ACCESS

This is a Divine Decree (A Supreme Universal Call) for all Good, Clean and Able Moors throughout the world, including Churches, Mosques, Synagogues, Temples, Small and Large Businesses, Corporations, Academies, Organizations, Hedge Funds, Secret Societies, Bankers and Sovereign Expatriates, etc., to take your place in the Affairs of Nations and become recognized by the Nations of the Earth by Joining and Entering Nationalnomics for the Uplifting of fallen humanity, because it takes finance to uplift a Nation (Knowledge of Self + Love of Self & Others

=Energy in Motion [True Wealth], which is the formula of the Great Equation-W=F x D / Work=Force Times Distance).

This is the only reparations that the Moors (Asiatic Nations) will receive

In compound interest, as directed by the Holy Prophet Noble Drew Ali and the solution to our economical problems throughout the world as directed by the Supreme Master C.M. Bey (Charles Mosley-Bey).

"The Great Meeting Is On—This is the Uniting of Asia".

Act-3 and Act-6 of the Divine Constitution And By-Laws are in Full Effect;

Act-2 and Act—3 of the Additional Laws for Moorish Americans and Moorish Nationals are in Full Effect;

Amendment I (Sovereign Moorish Nationals); Amendment II (Tax Exemption); Amendment IV (National and International Trade); Amendment VI (Transportation); Amendment VIII (Rights of Accused Moorish Nationals) and Amendment IX (Moorish Rights to Commerce and Financial Access) of the Moorish Zodiac Constitution (The Great Seal) is in Full Effect and is being Fully Enforced in this Two Thousand and Fourteenth Year (2014).

Signed and Sealed

King Connally-Bey
Inpropria Persona Sui Juris
**Moorish-American/National
By Inheritance . . .**

Introduction

To

Bank

Debenture

Trading

Programs

An Introduction To Bank Debenture Trading Programs
Please Note:

This Is Not a solicitation, but for informational purposes only.

These documents are not in any form of bank offers or policy or on behalf of financial institutions and are not intended to be and must not be construed to be a solicitation of investment funds for a securities offering.

What Is A Bank Debenture Trading?

Bank Debenture Trading is not a new thing as it has been around for many years. However, with entry requirements starting at a USD $10 Million minimum and up, only the very wealthy and very connected were privileged enough to participate.

It has only been in recent years that the entry requirements have been made low enough and the knowledge of the trading has become unrestricted enough for a broader group of participants to enter and profit from the trading.

The following is an extract from information that explains briefly, how the exceptionally high investor returns common in these programs is possible.

In the U.S. the supply of money or credit is regulated by the Federal Reserve, an independent body that came into existence by an act of Congress in 1913 and in part by means of the authorization of certain key International Prime Banks.

Prime Banks comprise The Top 250 Banks Worldwide, as ranked by net assets, Long-term stability and sound management.

These banks are authorized to issue blocks of bank debenture instruments, such as Medium-Term Notes (MTNs) and Bank Guarantees (BGs) as well as Standby Letters of Credit (SBLC) for use in the Financial Markets or for Sale to Genuine and Confirmed Traders/Buyers who are purchasing on behalf of Secondary or Exit Buyers who have already entered into legally binding contracts and proven to have verified their Bank Funds to purchase the requested bank instruments.

The price for the requested Bank Instruments (usually with the face values of USD 100 Million or greater), are quoted as percentage of the face amount, and these Bank Instruments usually bear interest for a certain time frame such as 5 to 15 years in the case of MTN's (Medium Term Notes) or in the case of One Year Maturity BG's (Bank Guarantees) and SBLC's (Stand By Letters of credit) with zero interest rates.

There are no private procedures or terms and conditions within these types of transactions, there is only the International Bank to Bank Procedures, Regulations and Requirements and these Rules are strictly enforced by the people both within the system and the authorities who regulate the system, if the Buyers cannot or will not comply to these procedures, regulations and requirements, then they will not be able to acquire their requested Bank Instruments.

The initial market price is established by the Buyers requested volume to purchase and upon the issuance by the issuing Banks and their Traders or Providers depending on demand to buy and sell in the market and may be anywhere from 55% to 85% of face value for purchasing Bank Instruments, depending upon the type of instruments (Fresh Cuts, Slightly Season or Seasoned).

The quoted price will be based upon if the Buyer is buying the Bank Instruments as a Funds First Fresh Cut or Slightly Seasoned or Seasoned Bank Instrument and this will be done under a Contractual Bank to Bank structure which is the only method used by the Traders, issuing Banks and the Providers of these Instruments.

Therefore, once issued, the Bank Instruments are then sold and resold down the money market chain to retail at escalating prices at each transaction, thus realizing a higher profit on each transaction, which can be as little as one day to complete if all parties have proven their ability to pay and deliver as per the normal International Banking Procedures and Security Requirements.

As an Example: A Trader Working with the Top Banks, Who by Legal Agreement, Is Empowered to Receive and Place the First Issue Of a Bank's USD$100 Million instruments and who has a waiting supply of end retail buyers (Exit Buyers) usually Pension Funds, Hedge Funds, Trust Funds and Other Banks with Proven Bank Funds & Signed Contracts, can sometimes clear 6-10 percentage points ($6-$10M USD) or more per issue or transaction and a good Trader is capable of closing 1 to 2 trades per day, four days per week.

As These Returns Are Spread over a 40 Week Trading period, it is not difficult to understand why the investor, as the Capital Provider for the first initial Trade or Buy/Sell Transaction, receives such a high guaranteed rate of return for funding this operation.

Further, The Potential Buyer Needs to Understand that the Trader will not undertake to buy or commit to The Bank for the issue of their Bank Instrument unless he has already a signed Legally Binding Contract in place for the resale to a Retail Buyer with Proven Bank Funds in hand so that the Investor's Capital and the Trader's Position are never put At Risk for any reason by any Exit Buyer who may fail or not complete the transaction.

The Trader will only use your investment as part of a fund to buy the first issue of the Banks Instruments at a very good discounted price and to then mark the price up and to on sell the Purchased bank Instruments to their contracted and proven exit buyer as detailed above and you as the investor will share in a percentage of the profits along the way for each trade completed.

The Profits are derived from the Difference between the Discounted price that the Trader pays to the bank for their initial Issue and the price he on sells to the Buyer.

The Prime Banks, on the other hand, are happy to receive your money for the Discounted sale of a Bank Debit Note that is due to be paid in 5 to 15 years in the future and the cash paid is always backed by the value Of the Bank Instrument Purchased so the Investors Funds Are Never at Risk.

The Banks Will Use Your Cash Funds that has paid for the Bank Instruments Issued over the next one-five-to ten years to make profits and to roll up enough Cash Funds to pay for the Bank Instruments full value when it is presented back to the bank at maturity for full payment to the Current Owner.

The Banks participating in the Trading Program also get a percentage share of the trading profits as well.

Typically, the Trader, Bank And Program Manager Get 50% of the profits generated, with the balance going to the Investor, Broker and Representatives.

Example Only:

The Trader Will Purchase The Issuing Banks Initial USD 100 Million Bank Instruments at a Discounted Price of 40% to 50% Of the Face Value (USD 40 Million to USD 50 Million) using their Investors funds.

The Trader Will Then sell to the Exit Buyers on a funds first fresh cut or whatever the mode the paper currently is in basis at a legally Contracted Price of 65% to 85% plus the 2% agents fees, thus giving the Trader an immediate 15% to 35% profit Margin on each Transaction and as stated the Trader and the Bank will take their percentage share and the Investor will get the balance.

1. This 15% to 35% Percentage Value in Dollars depends upon the value of the Bank Instrument being purchased at the time, for instance, a USD 100 Million Paper Will Yield a Profit of say USD 15 Million to USD 35 Million, but a Bank Paper of USD 500 Million will yield USD 75 Million to USD 175 Million to split 50/50 between the parties.
2. Therefore, it is clear to see on a large contract quite a lot of profit is involved for all the parties, therefore they undertake this transaction using strict procedures to ensure that this transaction is successful and all parties receive their due share (profits).
3. Therefore, if the Trader is a good trader and is completing 2 Transactions or Trades per day, four days per week, then the Investors estimated return on Investment per week is a minimum of 60% prior to the profit sharing and if the Investor Invested USD 10 Million with the Trader, they would be receiving back USD 3 Million per week for 40 weeks giving a total return of USD 120 Million against an initial USD 10 Million Investment after the profit-sharing.
This type of Trading Is Unlike a Derivative (stock, bond, commodity) investments, where the hedging (an attempt to reduce market risk) of trades provides an element of risk and the returns are also not that substantial or guaranteed.

These Trade Programs Involves Interest-Bearing Bank Notes From Prime Top 250 World Bank's And These Notes Are the Product In a Series Of Daily Buy and Sells that Are Pre-Confirmed, Via Signed Legally Binding Contracts Prior To Each Trading Day.

The Following Information Referred to Herein with Regards to Private Placement Programs That Are Provided by Established Trading Groups and Trading Platforms and Facilitated through Recognized Top World Bank's Is Supplied to the Reader As Information Only for Educational Purposes and Is Not to Be Considered in Any Way to Be an Offer or Solicitation for Investment of Any Kind and at Any Material Time Whatsoever by Any Party.

Private Placement Trading Programs:
A Method of Bank Secured Asset Enhancing and Debt Free Project Funding...

This Is an Invitation Only Investment Structure, There Are Strict Requirements And Procedures to be followed in order to be invited and to enter into These Investment Structures, As Is the Security Checking And Verification. Process of All Applicants and Their Submitted Documentation Must Clearly Pass Compliance.

Potential Qualified Investors:
Accredited Security Cleared Individuals, Project Principles, Business Corporations, Foundations, Trusts, Hedge Funds, Venture Capitalists, Pension Funds, Family Offices, Not-For-Profit Organizations, and Investment Managers can benefit from accessing a comprehensive array of Private Placement Solutions that would Empower them to securely and quickly to achieve their capital raising objectives.

The following advantages and benefits are available to the approved and qualified investor participants once they have completed all necessary documentary and banking requirements for their application for entry into the private placement programs and both they and their funds or assets have undergone strict and through security checking and verification procedures and processing has been approved for invitation into the Trading Programs (This Is Considered Passing Compliance).

With a one- time bank instrument buy/sell investment, within an investment period of 40 weeks, Project Principles could fund their projects for up to 100% of the costs, Debt Free within a secured and Structured Investment Mechanism.

In addition to Project Principles, this funding option could be very beneficial for any Business Corporation or Venture Capitalists with small or large projects that need to have a structured cash-flow over the life of their project or a project that needs to be quickly funded for fast-track construction and completion.

These Managed Investment Trading Programs create an immediate structured cash-flow that can be allocated to the project to fund all requirements of the project within the time frames required in a secured, orderly and timely manner with a potential residual balance of funds that can be used for additional projects.

Individual Investor Participants could greatly enhance their own cash assets with profit returns historically impossible in more commonly known investments such as stocks, futures, bonds, mutual funds and other commonly known investments that all have some degree of risk for the principal funds and the profit returns that are not very substantial and in some cases require extended time frames to achieve.

The Investor Participant would upon approval of their application for entry into the programs be invited to deal directly with some of the most established and active Trading Groups, Trade Platforms and Trade Banks in the International Banking Industry, thus assuring the best professionalism, management and security throughout the agreed contracted lifespan of the proposed trading transaction.

The Investor Participants keeps control of their invested funds for the duration of the investment period (est. 40 Weeks) because the funds can remain in the participants own current bank account (must be a Top 25 Bank).

If the funds have to be moved to a more recognized bank or the trading bank, then the new bank account would be opened by the Investor Participant himself in the participant's sole name only.

The funds will always stay in the participants own designated sole signature non-depletion account for the duration of the investment period as per the legally binding contractual agreement with the trading group.

When trading is conducted on behalf of the Investor then the Trader will act with the authority of the Investor to make the Trading Arrangements on behalf of the Investor.

Investment Managers, Brokerage Firms, Pension Funds and Hedge Funds Managers can through these programs access some of the best structured and proven financial solutions with excellent secured profit returns for both their and their clients investments with confirmed no risk factors.

Likewise, Financial Planners, Accountants, Attorneys as well as Business and Project Funding Brokers could access these secure and profitable bank instrument buy/sell private placements for their clients who are prepared to follow the International Banking and Traders application procedures and documentary requirements for security clearance and approval for entry into the program.

This Investment Trading Structure Would Be Done As Follows:

This is a basic format example only on how it would be structured for a Client and he can request assistance from the Consultants for a fee for his side of the transaction to be structured as required:

The Investor Organizes a Corporation (New Co) in a jurisdiction of his choice or an existing company or account;

The Investor will own all of the stock and New Company;

The Investor then opens a bank account at a top 25 World Bank of his choice;

The bank must have an active and operational Securities Department;

The Investor deposits approximately 500,000,000 USD or cash line of credit totaling 500 Million into the banks Premier Bank Account;

The Investor is sole Signatory to the Premier bank account;

The Investor Informs His Bank Officer That He Intends to Enter into a Purchase Agreement with a Well Known Trading Company;

This group that the investor will be dealing with specializes in trading Medium Term Notes (MTN's) and Bank Guarantees (BG's), herein after referred to as instruments. Due to the purchasing power of the trading company and their relationship with numerous banks throughout the world, they have access to instruments that are fresh cut, slightly seasoned and seasoned, however they have strict business procedures.

By Mutual Consent and legally binding agreements, the intent of the Investor and the Trading group is to enter into an Asset Management Agreement in which the Investor permits the trading group to utilize the Investors funds and access the trading groups purchasing power and to purchase instruments at wholesale pricing.

Procedures:

Duties and Responsibilities of Investors:

1. Establish a Single purpose Corporation domiciled outside of the United States;
2. The Investor will own all stock in the new Corporation;
3. The Investor will open a Premier bank account at a bank of his choice;
4. The Investor deposits 100,000,000 to 500,000,000 cash or cash line of credit totaling 100 Million to 500 Million into The Premier Bank Account, the largest amount of cash or cash lines of credit is preferred;
5. The Investors chosen bank must have an active Securities Trade Department;
6. In choosing a bank, the Investor should negotiate to have the bank give him some leverage against his cash deposit to increase the funds available;
7. The Investor must have a clear understanding with his bank and the bank's agreement based upon the intent of the proposed Profit Participation Agreement between Investor and Trading Group;
8. The Investor enters into a Profit Participation Agreement with the Trading Group;
9. The Investor must instruct the bank that the Trading Group must manage the Investors Account on a non-depletion protocol which the bank must agree to and abide by at all times;
10. This Premier Bank account can and will only be used for the purchase of bank instruments and NO other use is allowed under the legally binding Trade Agreement.

Duties and Responsibilities of Trading Group:

1. Access instruments at wholesale prices to be delivered into Investors account;
2. Cause all purchase of instruments to be under The Investors name and Investors bank coordinates;
3. Instruct the Investors bank to screen the instruments, verify and authenticate prior to paying for the instruments;
4. Upon authentication of the instruments, supervise the settlement via. Brussels Euro Clear with Investors bank.

Duties and Responsibilities of Trading Group: Cont.

5. Issue resale invoices to purchasers arranged by the Trader. All purchases will be resold and invoices issued to buyer within twenty-four (24) hours of investors bank showing receipt of ownership in the investors name;

6. Cause payment of the resale instruments to be deposited into the Investors Premier bank account;

7. Instruct the bank to credit Investors original purchase price to his account, deduct bank transaction charges and intermediary fees, if any. _The net remaining amount is to be disbursed between The Investor and the Trading Group's respective accounts as designated;_

8. Maintain Investors Bank Account at All Times Based upon a Non-depletion protocol. Either cash or instruments worth more than the cash paid out will always be in the investors account;

9. The Trading Groups maintains a group of approximately 40 buyers who are ready, willing and able to purchase instruments within hours of a receipt of invoice from investors account;

10. Historically a Profit Margin on Average, yields double digit returns per trade.

Duties and Responsibilities of the Bank:

1. Open a non-depletion account for Investor and agreed to furnish a Securities Trade Account;

2. Arrange a Margin Account for the Investor to increase his purchasing power;

3. _Agree to permit the Investor to purchase instruments issued by top twenty-five (25) World Bank's and assist the trading group in the settlement and resale of the instruments from the account;_

4. Verify, authenticate and settle each purchase via Brussels Euro-clear screen or ledger to ledger;

5. Cooperate with the Trader to issue Irrevocable, Conditional, Bank Pay Order (ICBPO) or in some instances, a Swift MT-103/23 for not more than the first three (3) tranches of any purchase of instruments, after which the Irrevocable, conditional bank pay order will be canceled and all future purchases will be conducted on a screen/block and pay protocol until termination of the Investor/Trader contract with third-party sellers.

The Application requirements to be invited to enter into these types of Investment Trading Programs are very strict and non-negotiable and they are inclusive of the Bank to Bank Proof of funds or Banking Asset (SKR/MTN/BG/SBLC) to be used as the Investment Capital, full disclosure of the Investors details (Clients Information Sheet) and their Passport Copies are required, for there are very stringent security checks carried out on both the Investor, their funds, the source of the funds and the proposed use to which the program profits will be put to use once the investor starts to receive their net profits.

These Private Placement Programs are designated as "Reserved Funds" (meaning that the Investors Capital Funds will remain in participants sole signature account). The Private Placement Trading Programs usually starts with investment capital of $10 Million USD and up.

Once the Investor has submitted their application through the designated procedures and the application has been processed and the applicant has been approved and invited for entry into the Private Placement Programs, the Trading Group and their Banks will deal directly with the Investor for the structuring of the Investment Contract and the Participant Investor will personally finalize his or her investment agreement directly with the Trading Group, and signs his or her own contracts.

The entire investment is transacted with no Trust or Escrow accounts, and No Upfront Cost or Fees other than what the Investor is required to pay to his consultants for their time and efforts, however, there are certain Profit Sharing Percentages that the Investor will be required to agree upon with the Trader and their agents and these Profit Sharing Percentages will be detailed under and within The Legally Binding Contract and the Investor Is Required to Pay their own representatives a fee out of the net Profits paid to the Investor.

Typically the Participant starts receiving profit returns within 15 International Banking days from the actual signing of the legally binding Investment Contract with Trading Group and every week or month thereafter as per the agreement terms of payment contained within the Investment Contract for the agreed duration of the trading contract.

GLOSSARY OF TERMS

The definition of terms used in the industry is presented below:

Best Efforts - A destination that a certain financial result is not guaranteed, but that a good faith effort will be made to provide the results that are represented.

Bond - Any Interests-Bearing or Discounted Government or Corporate Security That Obligates the Issuer to pay the holder of the bond a specified sums of money, usually at specific intervals, and to repay the principal amount of the loan at maturity.
A secured bond is backed by collateral, whereas an unsecured bond or debenture, is backed by the full faith and credit of the issuer, however, not by any specific collateral.

Collateral Provider – An entity which has the contractual ability to purchase bear instruments directly from the issuer.

Also Known As Master Collateral Commitment Holders:

Conditional S.W.I.F.T - A method which uses the Society for Worldwide Interbank Financial Telecommunications to transfer funds conditionally between banks subject to the performance of another party.

Contract Exit for Non-Performance - A condition in a financial agreement that enables the investor to take back his funds if the result represented is not achieved.

Debenture - A general obligation backed only by the integrity of the borrower, not by collateral. Depository Trust Corporation (DTC): A domestic custodial clearing facility owned by all of the major banks and securities firms which are monitored by various banking regulatory agencies and the Securities and Exchange Commission.

Draft -A signed written order by which one party (the drawer) instructs another party (drawee), to pay a specified sum to a third-party (payee).

FORFAITING - The process of purchasing at a discount registered bank "paper" which will mature in the future without recourse to any previous holder of the debt-generated bank paper.

Glass-Steagal Act - *A portion of the Banking Act of 1933 which prohibits banks from entering into the securities business and prohibits securities firms from accepting deposits.*

However, any security which is issued or guaranteed by any bank is not subject to the Security Act of 1933.

Therefore bank instruments, by virtue of being issued by a bank, are not considered a form of securities.

International Chamber of Commerce (ICC) - An international body which governs the terms and conditions of various financial transactions worldwide, it is headquartered in France and has no affiliation with the local Chamber Of Commerce offices.

Key Tested Telex (KTT) – An older form of transferring funds between banks using a Telex machine on which the messages are verified by use of key code numbers.

Leveraged Programs -Programs which use leased assets (such as United States government obligations) to increase the amount of instruments purchased and resold for a profit.
The benefit of leased assets is that such programs generate substantially larger profits.

Medium-Term Note (MTN) - When discussing bank trading programs, a standard form of debenture with a term of 10 years and an annual interest rate of 7.5%.
Also known as Medium Term Debenture (MTD).

MT 100 Field 72 - A means of irrevocably transferring funds between banks using computers.

Off-Balance Sheet Financing - The process where the liability is contingent (depending on certain events). It is not listed as a liability, but typically appears in the Notes to the financial statement of the party.

108% Bank Guarantee - A written guarantee issued and payable by a bank which provides for the return of the principal amount and eight percent (8%) interest.

One-year Zeros – *An obligation of a bank due in one year and sold at a discount from face value in lieu of an interest coupon.*

Par - *Equal to the nominal or face value of a security.*
A bond selling at par is worth the same dollar amount as it was issued for, or at which it will be redeemed at maturity.

Parallel Account - *A separate account established at the transactional bank.*

Pay Order - *Document which instructs a bank to pay a certain sum to a third-party.*
Such orders are normally acknowledged by the bank which provides a guarantee that the payment will be made.

Safekeeping Receipt (SKR) - *A document issued by a bank which obligates the bank to unconditionally hold certain funds separate from other bank assets and return them when requested by the depositor.*
In this way, the funds are not an asset of the bank nor are they directly or indirectly subject to any of the banks other obligations or debts.

Sub Account (Segregated Account) – *Where an entity has established a relationship with a bank that includes the bank acting on the entities behalf, a sub account is opened to hold funds in the name of the entity's client.*

The funds can only be used according to the terms of a written agreement that is given to and approved by the bank.

The funds are not considered an asset of the entity or the bank, and are not subject to the debts of either the entity or the bank, if a safekeeping receipt is issued by the bank.

Tranches - *A specified part of a larger transaction.*

Each purchase and resale of a separate block of bank instruments in a trading group is known as a tranche.

For example, a contract may be signed to buy $10 billion dollars worth of bank paper with an initial tranche (or purchase) of $500 million dollars.

BACKGROUND
From The
US
FEDERAL
RESERVE
FOR
DEBENTURE
TRADING
PROGRAMS

INTRODUCTION TO BANK DEBENTURE TRADING PROGRAMS

1. _WHAT IS A BANK DEBENTURE TRADING PROGRAM?_

Also referred to as a Secured Asset Management Program, this is an investment vehicle, commonly used by the very wealthy where the Principal Investment is fully secured by a Bank Endorsed Guarantee and the Principal is managed and invested to give a guaranteed high return to the Investor on a periodic basis with no risk of losing the Investors Principal Investment Funds.

This Investment opportunity involves the purchase and sale of Bank Debentures within the International Market in Controlled Trading Programs, Whereby the Trading Program Allows the Investor to Place His Funds through an established Trading Program Management Firm or Trading Platform who are directly working with a Major Trading Bank.

The Investment Funds are secured by the Banking Institution at the time the funds are deposited and the Investor is designated as the Beneficiary of the Guarantee Unless Otherwise Instructed by the Investor.

The Investor is also guaranteed by the Program Directors and by the contract that they will receive with what is in effect a percentage of each trade made by the Trade Bank and this therefore is the form of the guaranteed profit/yield paid to the Investor on a periodic basis under the terms and conditions of the signed contract.

The Instruments are a Debt obligation of the Top One Hundred (100) World banks, in the Form of Medium Term Bank Debentures of 10 years in length usually offering 7.5% interest or "Standby Letters of Credit" of one year in length offering no interest, but at a discount of the Face Value of the Instrument.

These Bank Instruments conform in all respects with the Uniform Customs And Practice for Documentary credits as set forth by the International Chamber Of Commerce Paris France (ICC) in the latest edition of the ICC Publication 400 (1983 Revision) and the newest implemented ICC Publication 500/600 (1995 Revision).

2. _What Is the Investors Risk in This Program?_

As clearly demonstrated, the Investment Funds Principal is or can be fully secured by an Insurance Wrap if required which is issued by the Trading Bank at the time that the funds are deposited into their bank for the contract period, however the Investor is fundamentally secured from the start as the funds are deposited into an account in the bank under his own name and signatory and the Traders are only using these funds as the base collateral for the issuing and selling of the Bank Instruments and the real payment for the instruments is made by the actual Exit Buyer who is buying the paper.

This is why the bank and the traders have very strict procedures and requirements in place when dealing with any potential buyers who are all required to provide bank to bank proof of their funds to undertake the proposed purchase prior to any papers being issued out for sale or any instructions given to the bank to issue.

All elements of the risk have been addressed and it must be stressed that before an instrument is purchased, a legally binding contract is already in place for the resale of the Bank Debenture Instruments, therefore the Investors funds will never be put at risk.

The Trust Account, always remember, because the Trader and the Investor are buying at a discount and then reselling at a much higher price. There will always be either the funds or Bank Instruments of equal or greater value than that originally deposited into the Investors Account and after each transaction period, the profits are distributed according to the trading agreement and the process repeats for the duration of the contract.

3. _How Often Does The Trading Program Do Transactions?_

Operations will take place approximately 40 International Banking Weeks per year with specific transactions taking place one or more times per week, depending on the circumstances. Although there are 52 weeks in the year, there are only 40 International Banking Weeks during which the transactions take place and an International Banking Week is a full week which does not include an officially recognized holiday, however transactions can still take place in a short week containing a holiday.

4. *Why Are These "Secured High Return" Programs Not Advertised?*

These programs have been available though not widely known about for many years, but because of the extreme privacy and high minimum requirements to enter, only a few individuals ever qualify. The program have also been the basis of many scams by fraudulent individuals or joker brokers who know little about the programs, but do not have direct access to the actual individuals that are operating the system of the program, thus in many cases are again themselves just dealing with other joker brokers which are simply taking upfront fees for entry into the programs and then failing to deliver to the Investor the offered service which has made many Genuine Investors Very Weary.

The minimums of real cash funds that are free to be invested of USD $10 Million to USD $100 Million and up to USD $500 Million are not as readily available for investment as people would think.

In addition, there are security checks that the Investor has to undergo which are very strict security clearances to qualify for invitation and for entry into the programs, and as there are a number of people queuing to get invited into each of the individual programs, the quota for entry can be filled very quickly. There is only limited opportunity to gain invitation for entry.

The applicants are not only check for their security clearances and funds sources, they are also judged on their attitude and approach discussions to and with the Traders. There are many individuals which includes the Investors, their own Representatives, Mandates and Consultants that believes because they have the funds, think and believe that they do not have to follow or comply with any of the required procedures or documentary requirements and believe that they can dictate to the Traders, to the Trade Platform and to the Banks. It is these individuals that usually get an automatic rejection and in turn make complaints because they did not receive an invitation into the Program.

This is a privilege that very few are given and will ever earn. Having the funds does not give automatic invitation into the Programs.

High Yield Investment Program

1. _Background Of the Mechanics Of Prime Bank Guarantees (SBLC & BG):_

The US Dollar is the basis of the Worlds liquidity system since all other currencies base their exchange rate on the dollar and quite simply this means that the US Is the World's Central Banker.

Management of the US Dollars in circulation both in the US and abroad is the responsibility of the Fed and the Federal Reserve System founded in 1913 by an Act of the U.S. Congress.

The Fed's domestic tools for regulating the supply of money and credit are Interest Rate Policy, Open Market Operations, Reserve Ratio Policy and Moral Persuasion, but these tools are not always as effective as the Fed would like them to be.

Part of the reason for the less than perfect effectiveness is due to the substantial stock Of US Dollars in foreign jurisdictions where several of the Fed's tools or systems cannot be used in other countries, for example, the Fed cannot change Foreign Reserve Ratios.

Furthermore, a significant amount of credit creation occurs in US Dollars in foreign countries particularly in the Eurodollar Market, and as the World's Banker the US has an enormous responsibility to maintain the stability within the Worlds monetary systems.

The Federal Reserve Board (FED) uses two financial instruments to control and utilize the amount Of US Dollars in circulation internationally known as Standby Letters Of Credit (SBLC) and Prime Bank Guarantees (PBG).

Internationally the Currency of choice is the US Dollar as it is considered the safest currency especially in times of political crisis and consequently those holding the dollar, do so for reasons which are less sensitive to economic stimuli.

Background from the Federal Reserve

Because foreign banks readily accept US Dollar Deposits, those funds which in the domestic contexts are the basis of the M1 Money Supply Act; in the foreign context more like the near money features of M3, which means that they are much more difficult to control.

The Offshore market has grown substantially in the past two decades for a number of reasons. First, huge amounts of US Dollars associated with the Drug Trade, slosh around within the International Monetary System, and second, wealthy individuals concerned about high taxes and preserving their wealth opt to keep their assets in off-shore tax havens.

Therefore this significant stock of US Dollars cannot be controlled effectively by the US using their normal domestic policy tools.

Lastly, Currency Futures Markets can be another difficult area to control because of the substantial amount of leverage that is available in the market.

For Example:

For as little as USD $1,500 it is possible to go short or go long in the market for a block of USD $150,000 versus the D Mark with all other Major Currencies having a similar leverage against the US Dollar.

This means that someone with USD $1,500 can take the other side in a FED move to stabilize the currency and since the currency does not have to be delivered as the contracts are rolled near the expiration date, it is possible to create substantial pressure on the US Dollar in either direction. (The Hunt Brothers found this out when they tried to corner the silver market)

To control the US Dollars outside the US, the FED resorts to Standby Letters Of Credit or as they are popularly known "SB LC".

Background from the Federal Reserve

In its more familiar domestic form, the SBLC is a financial guarantee or performance bond issued by a bank, for a fee on behalf of a Client that wishes to borrow funds but is unable to do so cheaply.

The Bank guarantees the borrower's financial performance to the lender by issuing the SBLC and as the bank is in a better position to assess the credit risk of the client and to demand collateral for the issuance of this type of guarantee, it is a natural service of the bank that it provides.

In the International Markets, the use of the SBLC is somewhat different as it is a money raising device where the financial guarantee is meaningless as the banks issue these SBLC on behalf of the FED, therefore in other words, the FED is the Client of the bank and obviously there is no credit risk, and by using this method the FED can reduce the Dollars in circulation in Foreign Jurisdictions.

Using a different method, the large stock of expatriated dollars is employed by the Fed to promote US Foreign-Policy.

For Example:

During the G7 Meeting in Tokyo in April of 1993 the US committed financial aid to Boris Yeltsin to the tune of USD$6 Billion, but these funds did not come from the US Treasury nor is the merit of the loan debated in the House of Congress, instead the US taps the International Pool of US Dollars through an Instrument called a "Prime Bank Guarantee" (PBG).

Especially a PBG, has the features of a SBLC except it can be longer in maturity up to 20 or 30 years, and unlike the SBLC which sale at a discount and bear no interest, the PBG can have a yearly interest rate and like the SBLC it is a form of guarantee ensuring that the lender will receive interest as it is due and be repaid the principal upon maturity.

It is important that the US has these tools to control the Dollars that increasingly grow off its borders as the FED operates its currency stabilization so effectively through the use of the SBLC's, that it seldom results to intervening in the Foreign Exchange Markets.

Rather than the US Government tapping into the Domestic United States Savings Pool to assist foreign governments, it is able to tap into the International Pool of expatriated US Dollars that leaks away from its shores in hundreds of millions daily.

Background from the Federal Reserve

2. *The Institutional Structure of the System:*

A number of problems must be overcome to make the structure work successfully and inevitably the offshore US Dollars find their way into the International Banking System by way of deposits, therefore the International Banks must be the main buyers of any financial instruments the Fed causes to be issued.

However, the rules and regulations of the Bank of International Settlements (BIS), the bankers bank based in Basle Switzerland prohibits banks from buying the newly issued instruments from each other directly, and this prohibition exists for obvious reasons.

If banks were allowed to fund one another directly, then the probability of a system wide bank failure would be increased and this system of funding is not intended to support weak banks, in fact the opposite objective is the goal.

Therefore the methodology has been constructed that allows banks to buy each other's newly issued paper as the BIS rules and regulations do not prohibit the banks from owning other banks financial obligations, as long as they do not purchase the paper directly from another bank, but instead purchase the paper from the secondary market through very private and confidential sources.

The Fed Supports a Group of Intermediaries that have substantial available Cash Reserves for the intermediaries to Purchase Paper from the issuing banks and almost immediately resale it to the other banks; and it is these Intermediaries who are known as the "Commitment Holders or Providers". The Federal Reserve Board, Licenses a Small Number of Commitment Holders to participate in their quiet Confidential International Monetary Policy and these People are identified by Confidential FED issued Registration Numbers.

The Commitment Holders are few in number, however, they are very essential to the smooth running of the process and they are required to maintain the secrecy and privacy of the market and their operations at all times, no matter what the reasons, the Commitment Holders will often forge relationships with other sources of funds which are designated as sub-commitments, and holding a Commitment entails a number of conditions which are extremely important to maintain in order to keep the issued license, or risk termination of the license and the access to the market.

Background from the Federal Reserve

- *First and foremost there is the demand for the Individuals involved to maintain Utter Secrecy At All Times; Secondly, The Commitment Holders must be able to quickly produce large sums of US Dollars, generally in the Billions, and this factor explains why The Commitment Holder is willing to take on Sub-Licenses who must also follow the license rules and regulations to ensure a large supply of readily available funds and finally, this is always a "Funds First" Business Transaction.*

Nobody can buy the issued paper on credit and to ensure that this does not happen, a Commitment Holder will not enter a transaction if the Buyer has not or cannot prove their funds to undertake the transaction.

The FED as well has identified a tier of high quality banks usually the top 100 in the world which it authorizes to deal in the issued papers and the criteria for being on the FED's list, includes strength in the normal banking ratios, sound management, long-term stability as well as being in a country in which the FED desires to be active.

It is somewhat evident that the largest supply of International US Dollars is in Europe, which explains the dominance of the European Banks on the FED list.

Another aspect of this fund raising process is the fact that it is conducted entirely off the balance sheets of the issuing bank in both instruments, SBLC and PBG's are guarantees and as such, represent contingent liabilities, which as contingent liabilities they are not posted to the balance sheet.

However they do require a risk-adjusted amount of capital reserve as prescribed by the BIS rules and regulations and by keeping the funding instruments off the balance sheets there is little if any disruption to the normal financing activities of the Banks.

3. Issuing Paper:

The Federal Reserve decides which banks will issue paper, what kind, how much, at what point in time, and who will handle the transactions. The United Nations and the World Bank also have similar authority with the PBG's, but they too must coordinate with the Fed.

A Commitment Holder and a bank work together to operate a Trading Program whereby the Commitment Holder, is the source of the funds to activate the paper and the bank establishes a list of other banks from which it will accept paper.

The list reflects the preferences of the owner's of the funds who want the paper and obviously the strongest banks will appear on the lists with the highest frequency, which causes these banks to benefit the most from these activities.

The strongest banks attract the Commitment Holders to operate their Trading Programs from within their banks.

Banks do the actual trading and the Fed will inform them of who is issuing instruments and who wants to buy instruments. A buy and sell trade transaction will then be arranged.

They arrange the trades, verify and confirm the securities, and clear the trades. Throughout, the Commitment Holder is an integral part of the process, although it does not have to be present to make it function, as all they must do is leave the required amount of funds at the trading bank in a custody account after all of the procedures have been properly executed.

The Commitment Holder is the source of the funds that are used to purchase the initial issue of paper and immediately resale it to another bank or client, and due to this factor, there is no room in the system for anyone without the funds to undertake the transaction on a funds first basis, as this is a Principal To Principal (Bank to Bank) business only.

The Trading Bank executes the trades and finds the buyers for the issued papers; outsiders can only access the system through finding a Genuine Commitment Holder and lodging the funds with themselves or with one of his sub-commitment holders. They are always searching for Genuine Investors with the cash funds to invest.

4. Why Are the Profits So High?

As the Investment does not appear intrinsically risky, how then are the high profits returns on these High-Yield Programs generated.

There are certain factors that contribute to the process of achieving the high profits. The International Market for the US Funds is extremely competitive.

For Example:

There are several countries whose desire for US Dollar funds is extremely high, so much so, that they are willing to pay annual interest rates of 20% to 25%, make monthly interest payments in US Dollars and to issue Debentures whose terms do not exceed one year.

These are countries whose risk profile is high, even though there is no record of default on their obligations and these are the borrowers who set the benchmarks at the high end of the interest rates, while at the other end, is the very low risk Sovereign Issuers who are able to attract funds at rates that are competitive with the US Treasuries rates.

Earlier it was explained, how the institutional side of the process functions and it was pointed out that when the SBLC is issued by a Foreign Bank on Behalf of the Fed, it had to establish a Capital Reserve, now recent changes to the BIS Rules and Regulations requires balance sheet entries to be included in the computation of the Banks Assets and Capital Adequacy Ratios.

Furthermore, these assets and all other assets must be weighed to reflect their overall risk making all Capital Adequacy Ratios to be risk adjusted and the SBLC fall into the 100% credit conversion factor rating to convert the off-balance-sheet items to an on balance sheet equivalent.

Background from the Federal Reserve

If the Banking Guidelines required the ratio of Total risk weighted assets (rwa) not fall below 8%, then the bank would have to reserve a capital of 8 cents in every dollar of SBLC exposure, meaning that if a SBLC of USD $100 Million is issued, the bank must set aside USD $8 Million in capital, but in reality the capital requirements are not that bad, because there are a number of other factors at work that lowers the marginal cost of the capital utilization.

The issuing bank will also load in a charge for providing the service, which could be up to two points (2%) and as we shall see, the banks are paid their fees at maturity or redemption.

Next there needs to be an interest spread which will motivate the large sums of Capital to sit in the custody account in US Dollars and this spread could be up to four points (4%) and is earned by the owners of the capital the Commitment Holder, and reflects the cost of the fund raising and the economic rent of the capital.

The next question is, why would the Fed be interested in paying these high profit rates to the investors, and the answer is that, it is not as expensive as it appears, due to the fact that when the SBLC matures, The Capital Reserve Is Released.

More importantly, the value of the process to the FED, should be clearly understood, as any country which is attempting to stabilize its currency and implements one or both of the following policies.

The first line of attack is to manipulate the interest rates to increase or decrease the flow of its currency by altering final demand and if speculation becomes too powerful, which it often does, the next line of attack is to intervene in the currency market to remove the excess supply or demand.

Changing interest rates can be disruptive enough, but once the speculators see a weakening or strengthening currency, then it becomes very expensive to rapidly correct the situation and as the US Dollar is the base currency of global commerce, the speculation can occur at very swift rates that are hard to keep pace with.

The cost to the global economy would be significant let alone the cost of the FED having to intervene in the matter, therefore from this perspective the manner in which the FED conducts its activities probably is not expensive.

Background from the Federal Reserve

There are countless examples of where a Central Bank has announced that it will defend its currency in USD $15 Billion later they give up, just as Britain did when it pulled out of the ERM in 1993 and that money goes into the pockets of the speculators.

The only perhaps negative aspect of this system is that the FED is reliant on a group of Fundraisers called Commitment Holders who grow very rich from the service that they provide on behalf of the Fed. However, the Fed has some control over them under their licensing rules and regulations and this is the only way and most effective way that the FED can keep the process Confidential and highly selective in its operations at all times.

There is a similarity in the Public Markets such as the New York Stock Exchange where Market Makers or Specialists are a very select club, which is extremely difficult to join.

Market Makers are charged with the responsibility of making markets in their particular stock by managing the balance between the supply and the demand, thus the Market Makers bear some risk, but it is one which is easily managed.

Market-Making Firms have the highest returns on Capital of any forms involved in the Stock Market and Commitment Holders are considered the same as Market Makers, though of a slightly different sort, as they do not bear any risk in making a market and their only risk lies in their ability to gather large amounts Of US Dollars (Funds) to be utilized in the Private Placement Programs, because unlike other Market Makers, they cannot leverage or monetize their capital.

The final question is why does the FED not issue these Securities directly to these banks to attract their Dollar Holdings?
First, the FED is not empowered to issue Securities, only the US Treasury Department and other agencies guaranteed by the US Government can do so, therefore the need for complete secrecy in the process is set and secondly, the selling of Bonds would be negatively perceived in the financial markets since they are generally used for deficit financing.

*The process works as well as it does because it is not visible
to persons who are not insiders of the system (what happens in Vegas, stays in Vegas).*

Only the issuance of a SBLC has been discussed so far and the issuance of a SBLC has the effect that it bids up the price of the Dollar, therefore if the FED is interested in injecting liquidity into an economy, then it simply repurchases the outstanding SBLC's in the Countries which it desires to lower the exchange value of the Dollar, which we will call this a "Closed Market Operation".

The domestic analogue of this foreign monetary policy is an open market operation in which Prime Bank Guarantees are used in the same way as they represent a financial guarantee and therefore are considered a contingent liability and unlike the SBLC, the PBG's are not used for currency operations.

These instruments support loans to countries and to development agencies which fund projects in LCD's and while PBG's are issued at bigger discounts than the SBLC's, they in fact have less interest rates and the reason for the bigger discount is caused by the fact that the PBG bears interest over a longer period.

For Example:

One point of discount on a SBLC equals 1.3 points of interest, while one point of discount on a PBG equals six points of interest per year, therefore it takes a larger change in the discount of a PBG to have the same effect on interest as the SBLC.

The economic consequences with a PBG are quite different than those associated with the SBLC as dollars are not removed from the system, they instead flow into areas where there is a perceived need to be philanthropic which is no doubt motivated by political considerations.

Once a Project has been initiated, the recipient of the funds begins to import materials and finished products which increases the amount of trade taking place, which in turn expands production and inevitably a large share of these Dollars is spent in the US.

Background from the Federal Reserve

The PBG is a method whereby the US can officially direct the use of its currency without explicitly saying that it is doing so, as the alternative would be to make it a budgetary expenditure which would need to be debated in the Congress and if it passed successfully through the process, then it would have to be added to the deficit of the country.

Such expenditure would most likely be funded by issuing New Government Bonds, and instead the issuance of PBG's is a more expedient way of accomplishing the same objective using the vast pool Of US Dollars deposited within the European banks instead of using the domestic Dollars.

The PBG does not appear to have any overt credit creation action as the stock of US Dollars utilized already exists in the economic system, however to the extent that a country defaulted on paying the PBG, then the FED would be called upon to honor its guarantee to the issuing Bank, which would cause credit to be created. Again the high interest rates are caused by the same reasons explained earlier and the discount rates will be larger to have the similar effect on the returns as the SBLC which results in the market participants making even more profit on the PBG issued.

5. Entry into a Trading Program:

This is one of the most secret and difficult areas that exists to invest into and there are many individuals around who knows certain aspects of the system, but very few who knows the whole system and because of this factor, there have been some individuals that have used this to operate scam operations to take the money of genuine investors.

This has prompted warnings from the Board of Governors of the Federal Reserve System and the controller of the currency as these scammers almost always attempt to set up their fundraising operations within the US and the Fed of cost will not have any of this, for the system was designated to control and utilize the Expatriate dollars, not the domestic dollars.

Let the record reflect, that Banks routinely deny the existence of these programs, even the Banks that are operating the programs, for they do not want to damage their Certificate Of Deposit Business, and the only way into the system is to be connected to the Commitment Holder or one of the Sub-licensees and to be able to show them Bank Certified and verifiable Proof of Funds for the required amount.

Finding or being able to apply to either one of these people is very difficult, as there are many more pretenders than there are legitimate Commitment Holders and the legitimate people always maintain a very low profile and will only operate according to the Rules, Regulations and Procedures issued to them by the feds and the banks with whom they operate.

In fact there is estimated to be only around 8 to 10 Genuine Master Commitment Holders in the world and if the investor cannot pass the security checks and provide genuine Bank Certified and Verifiable Proof of Funds in the form of cash or liquid collateral, then the chances of being accepted into the program is Zero.

6. *Successful Investment:*

The two elements for successful investing into the High-Yield Programs, is being connected to the right people to apply for access and to have the required funds for the investment that can be verified as real and to have the right attitude and be prepared to follow and comply with the required procedures at all times.

TABLE OF CONTENTS

It takes a Large Book to hide the Truth, it takes a small book to reveal the Truth.
moorishperpetualunion@aol.com

Salvation   Our God   Unity

The Moorish Perpetual Union

"The Inevitable"

Clock of Destiny Moorish Birth Rights

Great Seal Zodiac Constitution

National & International Club

Founded by C.M. Bey and Adopted by King Connally-Bey and Registered with Every Embassy and Government Agency throughout the World.

I   S   L   A   M

_____

The Universal Symbol of The 12 Signs of The Zodiac.

The Science of the Moorish Nation of The Order of Islam-North Gate.

(Clock of Destiny) Civilization. (The Law is Not a Secret).

The Star and Crescent

Flag of:

Freedom and Progress,

Human Equality, Justice   T. King Connally-Bey

and Peace. Culture.   A Free Moor, 3rd. 33rd and 360 Degrees

_____

Moorish-American Club Members Personal

Legal Document for Legal Defense in

The United States Court Room

Name:_____   Nationality: Moorish-American

By Inheritance

WARNING

This document Clock of Destiny Moorish Birth Rights is not bona fide without Club Membership (Clock of Destiny Card), Moorish Nationality Card, Clock of Destiny (Moorish Birth Rights) Zodiac Constitution of The Great Seal - the highest law of this land. And Seal impression and signature of T. King Connally-Bey, Publisher and Co-Author, Zodiac Constitutional Law Giver & Demonstrator.

BEWARE

This Publication (Document Holder)-the Members of this (Clock of Destiny) Club must bear in mind that they are under the highest moral and just law of this land - The Great Seal - and therefore must uphold its great moral, human and just

2

principles in all of their dealings. And do not entertain the thought that because you are not subjected to the Union States Magna Charta law of the land, you are free to violate it. Because you will be punished by your own Great Seal law. A crime is a crime universally.

JUDGE YOUR HONOR

With all due respect to this Court and to the men and women of the Bar Association of these United States of North America. I concede in the name of law, Truth and justice, that I, myself, cannot legally be tried in these 48 Union States Court rooms by said Union States law of the land.

HERE IS MY LEGAL PROOF

The present Union 48 States Municipal and Civil Laws Code of the Land is an Incorporated political unit of self-government established by the political powers of the General Assembly of each state of the union based on the Roman Catholic Church MAGNA CARTA Civil Laws Code in Philadelphia, Pennsylvania in the year 1854; which governs only the rights and conduct of the "White People" - Christians and Jews of the 1863 Union states right Republic under the Magna Charta K. of C. K.K.K. Oath: "To never allow the descendents of the defeated Moorish Nation of this hemisphere to ever become citizens of this Union States Republic".

UNION STATES PROPERTY

The Union states slave labels such as; Negro, colored, black, African, West Indian, Indian and African American caused the Moorish Descendents of North America and abroad to be ignorant of their inherited Moorish nationality and Zodiac Constitution of the Great Seal (Birth Rights).

Which makes them the segregated Jim Crowed (Stateless Persons) property of the Union states without citizenship rights and representation under the Union states (Magna Charta) law of the land.

Thus, upon the strength of this fact of the established law of the land.

I demand the Judge and the Prosecutor of this Court to present the State and also the said United States Constitution from 1789 to 1863 and read it in this court and by it defy my statement and also my inherited Moorish Nationality Card and Zodiac Constitution.

Let the record reflect that this court cannot legally proceed with my case nor can the judge and the prosecutor of this court legally question me until the state and the United States Constitution has been presented and read in this court in defiance of my statement.

Therefore, I request the judge and the prosecutor to please confine this court to my legal demand of the statute and the United States Constitution to be read in this court.

NEW
ORDER

Universal Symbols of the 12 Signs of the Zodiac. The Science of the Moorish Nation of the Order of ISLAM-North Gate. Clock of Destiny Civilization (The Law Is Not A Secret)

The Star and Crescent

Flag of:

Freedom, Progress,

Human Equality, Justice,

Peace & Culture. A Free Moor, 3rd, 33rd and 360 degree

This is the Zodiac Constitution for the Moorish Nation of North America, referred to as; Negros, Africans, Indians and Colored people, and "White" people and Jews.

This Constitution is the foundation of the Clock of Destiny, Volume I and II (Copyrighted by C.M. Bey and privately published, co-authored and distributed by T. King Connally-Bey).

BEWARE

NAME_____

PREVIOUS NAME_____

NATIONALITY: MOORISH-AMERICAN OR MOORISH NATIONAL

OCCUPATION_____

DATE OF BIRTH_____

Marriage by (This Constitution of the law of the Moorish Nation) Federal Identification or Computer Identification

_____

Article I.

The 12 Signs of the Zodiac and the Code of Mathematical Scaling from Zero to Nine (0 to 9), and the Science of Geometry (G), comprise the Constitution of the Living Moorish Nation of North America, referred to as, "Negroes", who Ruled the World and the Seven Seas by the 12 Signs of the Zodiac and the Science of Geometry (G), for Eleven Hundred and Ninety Six years, to the

(Amazon Dutch-German) Catholic Priesthood Fathers of the Revolution of 1789 and the Sisterhood Magna Charta, Emancipation Proclamation, Union Society of white supremacy in 1863, North America.

The 12 JURIMANS of the 48 Union States Society, and also the Nine Magistrates of the Supreme Court were founded upon the Moorish Nation 12 Signs of the Zodiac Constitution and Mathematical Scaling from Zero to Nine (0 to 9). Thus, without our Moorish Constitution, the Magna Charter-Emancipation Proclamation Union Society of the myth of white supremacy definitely could not have been founded in 1863.

ARTICLE II.

ZODIAC CONSTITUTION BIRTH RIGHT OF THE MOORISH-AMERICANS THE BEY'S & EL'S

Since the 12 Juryman's of the 48 Union states magna charter document of white supremacy and the nine magistrates of their Supreme Court were founded upon our Moorish Zodiac 12 Signs Mathematical Constitution. The lawmakers have no jurisdiction over the free Moors-Beys' and Els'- in the inherited land of the Moorish Nation, Namely: U.S.A., Canada, Central and South America.

The Moorish American nationality and their Sir Names-Bey and El, are their inherited birth rights without a legal due process of the lawmakers of the union society - U.S., because what our Moorish forefathers were, we are that today without a doubt of contradiction, namely-Moorish.

ARTICLE III.

TAXATION WITHOUT REPRESENTATION IS A SUPREME VIOLATION OF THE MOORISH NATION

The Moors, referred to as; Negroes, Blacks, Colored and African American, definitely can never become members and citizens of the union society of the 48 states. Therefore, they cannot be forced or drafted into the Union, U. S. Army or military service to fight for the magna charter code of white supremacy against themselves.

The lawmakers of the 48 States Union Order cannot force the Moors -The Beys' and Els', to pay taxes because taxation without representation is a supreme violation of the Moorish Zodiac Constitution Birthrights of Islam. When the union lawmakers denounce their immoral magna charter code, and resort to the Moorish Zodiac Constitution, then the Moors are compelled to pay taxes because every one of the nation will be equally represented by it. There is no room in the science of (Masonry-The Zodiac) for Mystic gods, religious worship, race, color, ignorance, war, crime, slavery and human injustice.

ARTICLE IV.

ADEQUATE EMPLOYMENT AND PROTECTION FOR THE MOORISH-AMERICANS

Every lawmaker and heads of industry and business enterprises of the 48 Union States Order are obligated members and citizens of the Magna Charter Christian Church and Temple System of Christ the King of the Jews; Meaning, Jury over the wealth and culture of the living Moorish Nation of North America.

Therefore, by the Moorish Zodiac Constitution, The Moors-Beys and Els, can demand adequate employment, food, clothing, shelter, medical care, equal rights and respect and protection from mob violence, rape and injustices; otherwise without being obligated to the union church and religious system of the order of Christ- the "White" Son Idol God.

ARTICLE V.

IMMORAL MARRIAGE LICENSE CODE AGAINST THE ZODIAC LAW OF NATURE

Truth cannot be altered and therefore need no apology and neither doctrine, because it is the supreme mental doctor itself, for the entire Human Family-Woman and Man.

(1) Thus the truth is that the Sisterhood Christian Daughters of the American Revolution-The (D.A.R.) established the marriage license states right code to prevent the Moorish men and women from marrying into their magna charter society of white supremacy.

(2) Did you ever stop to think that Woman and Man are all already married by the Supreme Law of Nature-and that a marriage license is a supreme act of violation of the law of nature? The natural law union between man and woman spells love and the reproduction of a child, which a marriage license

plays no part in.

(3) Definitely there cannot be any illegitimate children offspring from woman and man, because Woman is the Supreme Gate of Creation of both male and female children by the law of nature-which spells (I.S.L.A.M.) and I, Self, Law Am Master, The Carpenter and the Grand Architecture of the Human Family. "Adam" means the positive forces in Woman and Sons. And "Eve" means the negative forces of Woman and Sons, responsible for Evolution or Reproduction of children by the law of nature. The Pope, Priests, and Preacher, Magistrate of the Christian Society definitely cannot prove that their "Adam"and "Eve" had a marriage license. Did you ever stop to think that the marriage license code is an act of selling woman and man back to themselves? The union magna charter marriage license code unfortunately and unconsciously caused the "White" Woman to be cut off from the Human Family-The Moorish Nation. In other words, the "White" Woman are supreme social slaves against their will and desire. This has caused them to carry in their minds and heart a secret sorrow and anger which causes their children to inherit a tendency of crime, hatred, insanity and various other diseases.

I.S.L.A.M.

SUPREME STANDARD OF THE ZODIAC MARRIAGE LAW-CULTURE

The Element of the Signs of the Zodiac and Woman and Man's opposite signs and first marriage of the Zodiac Law of Nature. No preacher, money, license and neither religion is necessary in the standard Zodiac Marriage Law.

4. Cancer (120) is Water and Capricorn (300) is Earth.

5. Leo (150) is Fire and Aquarius (330) is Air.

6. Virgo (180) is Earth and Pisces (360) is Water.

The 1863 Union Bible Story "Eve" and "Adam" were founded upon the Moorish Zodiac 12 Signs Law-The Negative and the Positive Forces of Nature-Female and Male. Woman and Man's second marriage and the Element of the angles of the Signs of the Zodiac the standard Universal law.

IN HARMONY WITH NATURE

1. Aries (30) is Fire and Gemini (90) is Air.

2. Leo (150) is Fire and Libra (210) is Air.

3. Sagittarius (270) is Fire and Aquarius (330) is Air.

Persons entering in the physical form under the opposite signs and the angle signs are in harmony with one another in every manner. Thus, first-handed knowledge of the sign under which you and your mate were in the physical form, will guide your destiny in peace, progress and happiness forever. Let us remember this is not a theory. The zodiac is the absolute universal standard of marriage and human guidance. Woman and man will know their duty towards one another and their children without being forced by the traditional code of the court room.

ARTICLE VI.

THE ONE AND ONLY UNIVERSAL MORAL LAW FOR UNITY, PEACE, ECONOMIC AND SOCIAL PROGRESS

The Moorish Zodiac Constitution is the only Universal unchanged Moral Law for the human family, for unity, human equality, respect peace and economic and social progress. Therefore every Moor-The Beys' and Els', must be guided by this Constitution and Book "Clock of Destiny" and do that which is right by reason and have respect for the "White" Lawmakers and Citizens of the Magna Charta Union Society of the 48 States, in order to demand respect from them.

The "White" Peoples of the Union are guided by their Magna Charter Traditions and customs, while the Moors are guided by the Zodiac Constitution Law. Nevertheless, their customs and traditions including themselves must be respected by the Moors, without submitting themselves to any of the Magna Charta Customs. That which is termed the Christian Law is a rule of action recorded on paper and supported by authority and force. The Zodiac Law of Nature is recorded in the Wisdom of Woman and Man and supported by Moral Intelligence the Greatest Law (The Greatest Need-Common Sense). Knowledge of Zodiac Masonry as shown in this Moorish Constitution, and also in the book "Clock of Destiny" Volume I and II, will prevent a Moorish American (He or Her) from indulging in crime. They then would not have to appear in the court room to stand trial. Should a Moorish American who have this Constitution and Book I and II, indulge in crime, such as; Narcotics, Robbery, Forgery, Prostitution, Illegal Whiskey, or Alcohol, Illegal Schemes, Gambling, Peace Breaking, Domestic Violence and Disrespect For the Law of the City, County, State and Federal, they then have incriminated themselves and therefore will be penalized. This Constitution and Card and Book definitely do not protect criminals. Beware.

WARNING

The Clock of Destiny Moorish American Card of identification and Constitution has been registered in the Library of Congress and Signed by the Author, C. M. BEY. The Authorized Solicitors are; H. Coley-El, A. M. Bey, William Spearman-Bey, Leslie Ferrell-Bey, The Moorish National Order School of the Great Seal, The Moorish Perpetual Union Founded by Titus K. Connally-Bey whom Adopts The Great Seal Zodiac Constitution, The Articles Of Unification, All Authorized by Universal Supreme law.

BEWARE OF FORGERY OR IMPOSTERS

A Moorish American cannot be convicted on false accusations-frame up charges. The evidence against a Moorish American must be concrete proof beyond a shadow of doubt. The Moorish Nation of 150 Million of the U.S.A., shall Not Be Destroyed for Lack of Truth And Knowledge of the Law and Constitution of the Moors.

ARTICLE VII

THE MOORISH-AMERICANS FREEDOM AND LEGAL RIGHTS WHILE IN THE CHRISTIAN UNION COURT ROOMS

In the Christian Union Court Room, the Moors cannot be forced to remove their Red Fez from their heads, nor can they be forced to raise their hand and take an oath over the Christian Bible. Neither can the Moors-The Beys' and Els', employee "White" nor "Negro" Lawyers to represent them. The reason for this is that "White" People and their "Negro" Slaves definitely cannot represent Free Moorish Americans. The Negro Is the Property of the Union Slaveholders. The Moors must respect the court by saying "I Affirm". Here the court has no Jurisdiction over them Which Makes Them Automatically Qualified to defend themselves By Their Zodiac Constitutional Law and their Mathematical number Nine (9), the number Nine (9), corresponds with the letter I, Based on the Nine Months from Conception to Birth, which makes you, Yourself, "THE GREAT I AM", The First and the Highest Law of Self Protection and Self-Preservation in harmony with your Zodiac 12 Signs unchanged Constitution Moral Law of 360° Degrees Squared by your number Nine (9).

The Moorish Zodiac Constitution is referred to in Christian Mason mythology as, "The Holy Koran" or "Al-Koran", meaning Earth, Moon, Sun and the Planet's or the Chronology Zodiac Record of the Moorish Nation of the Northgate-North America. The Name "Mohammed", Prophet, Religion, God, Church, Temple and Mosque, were established by the Dutch-Angelo Saxon Priesthood Franciscan Fathers of North America who overthrew The Moorish Society of Islam between 1789 and the Union of 1863.

The Moors-The Beys' and Els', must never attempt to teach or lecture in the Christian Institutions, namely; Church, Temple, Mosque, School and Hall, this would Infringe upon the Union Society States Right Magna Charta Code of Mary and Christ. The Truth of the Moorish Zodiac Constitution Law and Moral Human Principle, definitely conflicts With the Christian Union Customs and Doctrine of the Magna Charta from every angle. Nor do not criticize the "White" Peoples beliefs in The Religion of their Son and Woman Image. Nor do not ever attempt to influence the "White" People to accept the Moral Truth and Principles of your 12 Signs Zodiac Constitutional Law, because the Magna Charta is a Latin phrase meaning, MAGNATE CHARTER of "White" Peoples Economic And Social Attraction Only, which had its beginnings in the Colonies of Ohio, Michigan, Indiana and Illinois in 1848 and 1854 and will end. (WA ALAIKUM AS-SALAAM) Moorish Latin, which mean; and With You Be PACE (ISLAM).

If the Lawmakers of the 48 Union States of North America should attempt to ignore the Moorish Americans Zodiac Law and Birthrights of this Constitution, it would be an act of supreme violation of their own Magna Charta Code.

A Son Of A Widow   SIGNED BY:

The Moorish System Of Great Learning

Planet	Angel	Cosmic Function	Spatial Bearing	Operations of the Spirit
Sun	Michael	Giving Light to World	Zenith	Will
Moon	Gabriel	Strengthen Hope (Visions)	Nadir	Imagination
Mercury	Raphael	Civilizes	Centre	Motion/Intuition
Venus	Amael	Love	West	Love/Fellowship
Mars	Samael	Destroyer	South	Action/Destruction
Jupiter	Zachariel	Organize(r)	East	Judgment/Command
Saturn	Oriphiel	Watch Over	North	Patience/Perseverance

In Astrology each planet rules a specific period of life, the moon, early childhood (4-7 years of human life), Mercury from (7-14/15), Venus rules from (15) to 21 thru 24 (Adulthood from Teenage hood) or from adolescence to adult. Mars rule the prime of life (35-42), 21-24 to 35 is ruled by the Sun. Jupiter rules from age 42 to 56 (The Essence of Life). The next 28-30 years is ruled by Saturn.

Mercury =Child,   Venus= Girl,   Jupiter= Grown Man,   Saturn=Old Man,

Moon=Full Grown Woman,   Sun= God Man or God (Enlightened) Head.

Jupiter= Ruler of the Spirit!

Surah 78:12- 19

INTERNATIONAL & NATIONAL CLUB

Founded by the Moors and Inherited and Adopted by Bro. Titus K. Connally-Bey, Revision Pursuant to Article VI, of the Zodiac Constitution.

Universal Symbols of the 12 Signs of the Zodiac

The Science of the Moorish Nation of the order of ISLAM-

Northgate, Clock of Destiny Civilization, Supreme Law

(The Law is not a Secret)

New Order

The Star and Crescent

Flag of:

Freedom, Progress,

Human Equality, Justice,

Peace & Culture.

A Free Moor, 3rd, 33rd and 360 Degree

Moorish-Americans Club Members Legal Document For Legal Defense in the

United States Court room.

Name_____Nationality: Moorish-American by Inheritance

ARTICLE I

Warning This Document Is Not Bona Fide without Club Membership (Clock of Destiny) Card, Moorish Nationality Card, Clock of Destiny (Moorish Birthrights) Zodiac Constitution with Moorish Declaration of Rights of the Great Seal-The Highest Law of the land and Seal Impression.

ARTICLE II

Beware the members of this (Clock of Destiny) Club must bear in mind that they are under the Highest Moral and Just Law of the land-The Great Seal, therefore must uphold its Great Moral, Human and Just Principles in all of their dealings. And do not entertain the thought that because you are not subjected to the Union States Magna Charta law of the land; you are free to infringe upon it. Because you will be punished by your own Great Seal Law. A crime is a crime universally.

ARTICLE III

Magistrate with all due respect to this court and the ladies and gentlemen of the Bar Association of these United States of North America, I stand In Propria Persona (Sui Juris), and Concede in the name of law, Truth and Justice, that I, Myself, cannot legally be Tried in these 50 Union States court rooms by said Union states law of the land.

ARTICLE IV

My legal proof is the Present Union 50 States Municipal and Civil Laws Code of the land is an Incorporated Political Unit of self Government Established by the Political powers of the General Assembly of each state of the union based on the Roman Catholic Church Magna Charta civil laws code in Philadelphia, Pennsylvania in the year 1854.

Which governs only the rights and conduct of the "White" People-Christians and Jews of the 1863 Union States Right Republic under the

Magna Charta Knight of Columbus Ku Klux Klan Code & Oath: Never allow the Descendents of the Defeated Moorish Nation of this hemisphere to ever become Citizens of this Union States Republic. Chief Justice Taney Decision, 60 U. S. (19 HOW), 393, 15 L. Ed. 691.

ARTICLE V

Union States Property, The Union States slave labels, such as: Negro, African, West Indian and Indian cause(d) the Moorish descendents of North America and abroad to be ignorant of their inherited Moorish Nationality and Zodiac Constitution of the Great Seal.

Which makes them the segregated Jim Crowed property of the Union states without citizenship rights and representation under the union states (Magna Charta) law of the land?

The Constitution of the United States of America, states, in Article 1, Section 2, clause 3, "Representatives and direct taxes shall be apportioned among the several states which may be included within this Union according to their respective numbers, which shall be determined by adding to the whole number of free persons, including those bound to Service for a term of years [Indentured Servants], and excluding Indians not taxed, Three-Fifths of all other persons"... Three Fifths of all other persons referred to Slaves and including those bound to service for a term of years referred to Indentured Servants who were Contract Workers (Free Moors-Immigrants) who were silently put into slavery after the United States government failed to honor the contracts for their many years of service (Unpaid Labor). This debt was contracted before the operation of the Constitution of the United States of America and extends as far back as the Articles of Confederation, America's First Original Constitution, under the First President, John Hanson-Bey (A Free Moor).

Article Six (6), Section 1, clause 1, of the Constitution of the United States of America, states, "All Debts contracted and engagements entered into, before the Adoption of this Constitution, shall be as valid against the United States under this Constitution, as under the Confederation". Based upon this fact, the Moorish Americans are entitled to indemnification and reparations by inheritance from the Obligated Members of the 48 Union States Society.

It has been said that Amendments XIII, XIV & XV abolished slavery, granted so-called freed slaves citizenship and eliminated the three-fifth formula. Has it?

The United States Constitution (Colonial Document) of the United (Union) States of America is the law of the land, meaning the entire Constitution represents the 'People'. So the Preamble which proclaims that,

"We the People of the United States in order to form a more perfect union, establish justice, insure domestic tranquility, provide for the common defense, promote the general welfare, and secure the blessings of liberty to ourselves and our Posterity, do ordain and establish this Constitution for the United States of America".

"We the People and Posterity" meant and means the Sisterhood Christians Daughters of the American Revolution the Magna Charta Knight of Columbus, the Ku Klux Klan and the Union States as a whole and Posterity means their offspring. Fait Accompli. This fact cannot be denied. Therefore, Amendment XIV (14), cannot constitutionally add on anyone other than "White People", Christians and Jews of the Union Society or it will violate Article 1, Section 10, and clause 1, of the United States Constitution which forbids ex post facto laws. So if the Posterity is the People and their offspring and the Constitution excluded Indians and Other Persons (Slaves), it will be an Ex Post Facto Violation to later try to add them both to the same documents in the form of Amendments. That addition would be extremely unconstitutional. Furthermore, the United States Supreme Court held, "the descendents of Africans who were imported into this country and sold as slaves, were not included nor intended to be included under the word citizens in the Constitution, whether emancipated or not and remained without rights or privileges except those which the government might grant them. Dred Scott v. Stanford, 60 U. S. (HOW) 393, 15 L.Ed. 691. Keep in mind, this case has never been overturned!

Amendment XIV (14), Section 1. [1868]

"All Persons born or naturalized in the United States, and subject to the jurisdiction thereof, are citizens of the United States and of the state wherein they reside. No state shall make or enforce any law which shall abridge the privileges or immunities of citizens of the United States; nor shall any state

deprive any person of life, liberty or property, without due process of law; nor deny to any person within its jurisdiction the equal protection of the laws".

The word Persons earlier in the same body of regulation or laws, meant subhuman 3/5 slave (Article 1, Section 2, clause 3). The question is, if it's in the same body of laws (rules and regulation upheld by force and Brutish Authority), what does it means in its latter form? Nonetheless, the word born, in accordance with the first Americanized English dictionary written by Noah Webster in 1828, refers to the word born as an English Settler, thus, upon the strength of this fact of the established law of the land, I Demand the magistrate and the State Legal Practitioner of this court to present the state Constitution from 1789 to 1863 and read it in this court and by it defy my statement and also my inherited Moorish Nationality Card and Zodiac Constitution.

The Accused sites further from: "Once jurisdiction is challenged it must be proven". Hagens v. Lavines, 415 U. S. 533, N-3.

Let the record reflect that maritime law is being administered at this time in Magistrate_____ Courtroom. And a said United States Constitution, Article III Judge or Magistrate is in the sit-His/her finances are being diminished: Taxes, Social Security, and inflations, etc... Therefore, he/she is De Facto-As Is! And he function under Amendment Fourteen (14), who presence I_____ am being illegally tried under. The 13th, 14th, And 15th Amendments came when martial law should not have been in existence. Because martial law had/has already been vanished, which in turn make these three Amendments invalid. The question again is, is this a Common Law Court or a Maritime Court?

Nevertheless, let us remember that this court cannot legally proceed with my case nor can the magistrate and the state legal practitioner of this court legally question me until the state and the United States Constitution has been presented and read in this court in defiance of my statement.

Therefore, I ask the magistrate and the state legal practitioner to please confine this court to my legal demand of the statue and the United States Constitution to be read in this courtroom. I Rest My Case

Martial Law - Exists when Military Authorities carry on Government or exercise various degrees of control over civilians or civilians authorities in domestic territory; suspend all existing civil laws, as well as the civil authority and the ordinary administrating of justice.

De facto - In Fact, indeed, actually. This phrase is used to characterize an officer, a government, a past action, or a state of affairs, which must be accepted for all practical purposes but is illegal or illegitimate.

De facto judge - A Judge who is operating under color of law but whose authority is procedurally defective, such as a judge appointed under an unconstitutional statute.

Contravene – 1. To violate or infringe; to defy. 2. To come into conflict with; to be contrary to. Contrary to law-illegal, unlawful conflict with established law. [Latin. Contra venire, to oppose].

Contravene Constitution - conflict between two different Constitutions- only the Attorney General can handle such issues. Contravene - to act or be encounter, to contradict. [Latin. Contra venire, to oppose].

Denizen - A Person granted certain rights in a foreign nation or living habitually in a foreign nation. Denization.

Guarantee Clause – 1. A provision in a contract, deed, or mortgage by which one person promises to pay the obligation of another. 2. United States Constitution Article 4, Section 4, under which the federal government ensures for the states both a Republic form of government and protection from invasion or internal insurrection.

Natural Origin - The Country in which a person was born or from which the persons ancestors came. This term is used in several antidiscrimination statutes, including Title VII of the Civil Rights Act of 1964, which prohibits discrimination because of an individual's race, color, religion, sex, or natural origin. 42 U.S.C.A., Section 2000 e-2.

Contract Clause - The Clause of the United States Constitution prohibiting States from passing any law that would impair (diminish) private contractual obligations.
U

Universal Symbols of the 12 Signs of the Zodiac,
The Science of the Moorish Nation of the Order
Of ISLAM-North Gate, Clock of Destiny Civilization,
Supreme Law
(THE LAW IS NOT A SECRET)

New Order

I S L A M

CM Bey
Founder

The Star
and Crescent
Flag of:

Amendment I. Sovereign Moorish Nationals

Enacted Pursuant To Article s II, IV & VI of the Zodiac Constitution
Sovereign Moorish Nationals are known also as Moorish-Americans & Moors.
The rights of Moorish Nationals are not to be denied by any governmental
policies. The Sovereign Moorish Nationals are not bound by any city, county,
state, federal, criminal or civil laws of the land. Sovereign Moorish Nationals
consists of the bearer of the suffixes: Al, Ali, Bey, Dey, & El. Moorish
Nationals authorized in this document have the power and authority to issue
nationality to the unconscious Moors.

Amendment II. Tax Exemption

Enacted Pursuant to Articles III & VI of the Zodiac Constitution
Taxation without representation is a violation of the Moorish Constitution.
Moorish Nationals are not required or responsible for any form of taxation,
such as: Property tax, Income Tax, Social Security tax, Custom Duties and/or
any form of taxation.

Amendment III. Right To Bear Arms

Enacted Pursuant to Article IV of the Zodiac Constitution
Sovereign Moorish Nationals have the right to protect themselves and
property. Moorish Nationals have the right to bear Arms concealed or
unconcealed. Moorish Nationals have the right to be safe at all times in their
person.

Amendment IV. <u>National And International Trade</u>

Enacted Pursuant to Articles IV & VI of the Zodiac Constitution
The Sovereign Moorish Nationals Have the Right to Conduct National and International Trade and Trade Agreements with Other Nations within and throughout the world and World Communities. Border searches are prohibited.

Amendment V. <u>Education</u>

Enacted Pursuant To Article VI of the Zodiac Constitution
The Sovereign Moorish Nationals have the right to confer Degrees of educational merit. Also, Moorish Nationals have the right to educate their children and themselves accordingly. The Sovereign Moorish Nationals Degrees can be combined and/or used to enter any University, especially in their inherited land of their forefathers, now called the United States of North America.

Amendment VI. <u>Transportation</u>

Enacted Pursuant To Articles III & IV of the Zodiac Constitution
The Sovereign Moorish Nationals have the right to travel freely throughout the Nation and World(s). They do not need any form of license, Visa or permit to travel. The Moorish Nationals are not mandated to pay tolls throughout the city, County, State, Country and/or world. All public transportation can be enjoyed free of charge by the Moorish Nationals.

Amendment VII. <u>Authorize Solicitors And Governmental Bodies</u>

Enacted Pursuant To Article VI of the Zodiac Constitution
The Authorized Solicitors and Governmental Bodies are: The Moorish National Order School of the Great Seal, the Moorish Federation and the Moorish Perpetual Union, which derives its Powers from the Moorish National Order School of the Great Seal.

Amendment VIII. <u>Rights of Accused Moorish Nationals</u>

Enacted Pursuant to Articles II, IV, VI & VII of the Zodiac Constitution
Moorish Nationals are not to be held for ransom or bound by any city, county, state or governmental facility. Moorish Nationals have the right to appoint Moorish legal Representatives as Counsel in any Courtroom.

Sovereign Moorish Nationals are entitled to due process of the Union Society law, in the Christian Union Court Room. The Moors cannot be forced to remove their Red FEZ, Black FEZ, Turbans or any other type of National Headdress from their heads, nor can they be forced to raise their hand and take an oath over the Christian Bible.

Amendment IX. Rights to Commerce and Financial Access

Enacted Pursuant to Articles IV & VI of the Zodiac Constitution

Sovereign Moorish Nationals have the right to financial credit and other forms of financial access in partial re-imbursement, for the occupied land of their Forefathers and "Without Recourse". Sovereign Moorish Nationals have an Alienable Right to build and live on any unused land and take over any abandon building by way of Eminent Domain. Sovereign Moorish Nationals have the option of being part and partial with Union Society.

Amendment X. Rights Not Listed

Enacted Pursuant to Articles I, II, & VI of the Zodiac Constitution

The Sovereign Moorish Declaration of Rights is not by any means a complete list of rights. Any Amendments or additions to this declaration of Rights must be agreed amongst the governmental bodies listed in the Moorish Constitution and in this Moorish Declaration of Rights. The Moorish Constitution And the Moorish Declaration of Rights under The Moorish Perpetual Union are registered with the Union (United) States of America out of respect, regardless to the fact of the United States of America Constitution being suspended or not suspended during any period of time.

The Moorish Perpetual Union

The Constitutional By-laws

Of

The Moorish Nation

Preamble

The Nation of Moors, a Sovereign Moorish Nation, the official languages of which is Arabic and Hebrew, forms part of The Great Amexem.

As a Moorish Nation, it also has as one of its objectives the achievement of Moorish unity.

Conscious of the need to integrate its actions within the framework of the National and International Organizations of which it has and still, aiming for to be an active and energetic member of humanity.

The Nation of Moors subscribes to the principles, rights, and mutual obligations arising from those entities.

Likewise, the Nation of Moors reaffirms its determination to work for the maintenance of Peace and security throughout the world. In the year of our independence (1947) and on this year of our Adoption and Confirmation of the Zodiac Constitution of the Great Seal in 2013. We Do Set down on record these Articles of Unification in order that we may promote better understanding about our Moorish Ancestry, provide for the accurate education of our people, to secure the blessings of liberty to ourselves and posterity; and to re-establish Moorish law under the guidance of "The Moorish Perpetual Union" and "The Moorish Federation".

We, the undersigned Wazirs (Delegates) of the Moorish Nation, do ordain and establish these Articles of Unification pursuant to the law of the Zodiac Constitution of the Moorish Nation of North AMEXEM (AMERICA), Article 6: (The One And Only Universal Moral Law For Unity, Peace and Economical And Social Progress).

The Moorish-Americans under The Moorish Perpetual Union do adopt The Great Seal Zodiac Constitution, The Articles of Unification, The Moorish Science Temple of America Divine Constitution And By Laws and Additional Laws for Moorish-Americans by Noble Drew Ali on this_____, Day of

_____2013.

Signed and Sealed Into Law

_____

Titus K. Connally-Bey (I AM)

Moorish National by Inheritance

The Divine Origin Of the Asiatic Nations

1. The fallen sons and daughters of the Asiatic Nation of North America need to learn to love instead of hate; and to know of their higher self and lower self. This is the uniting of the Holy Koran of Mecca, for Teaching and Instructing All Moorish Americans, Etc.

2. The Key of civilization was and is in the hands of the Asiatic Nations. The Moorish, who were the ancient Moabites, and the founders of the Holy City of Mecca.

3. The Egyptians who were the Hamitites, and of a direct descendent of Mizraim, the Arabians, the seed of Hagar, Japanese and Chinese.

4. The Hindus of India, the descendents of the ancient Canaanites, Hittites and Moabites from the land of Canaan.

5. The Asiatic nations and countries in North, South and Central America; the Moorish Americans and Mexicans, in North America, Brazilians, Argentinians and Chilians in South America.

6. Colombians, Nicaraguans, and the natives of San Salvador in Central America, etc. All of these are Moslems.

7. The Turks are the true descendents of Hagar, who are the chief protectors of the Islamic Creed of Mecca; beginning from Mohammed the First, the founder of the uniting of Islam, by the command of the great universal God - Allah.

The Beginning of Christianity

1. The foundation of Christianity began in Rome. The Roman nations founded the first church, of whom crucified Jesus of Nazareth for seeking to redeem His people from under the Roman yoke and law.

2. Jesus himself was of the true blood of the ancient Canaanites and Moabites and the inhabitants of Africa.

3. Seeking to redeem His people in those days from the pressure of the pale skin nations of Europe, Rome crucified Him according to their law.

4. Then Europe had peace for a long time until Mohammed the First came upon the scene and fulfilled the works of Jesus of Nazareth.

5. The holy teaching of Jesus was to the common people, to redeem them from under the great pressure of the hands of the unjust. That the rulers and the rich would not oppress the poor. Also that the lion and the lamb may lay down together and neither would be harmed when morning came.

6. These teachings were not accepted by the rulers, neither by the rich; because they loved the principles of the 10 Commandments.

7. Through the Ten Commandments the rulers and the rich live, while the poor suffer and die.

8. The lamb is the poor people, the lion is the rulers and the rich, and through Love, Truth, Peace, Freedom and Justice all men are one and equal to seek their own destiny; and to worship under their own vine and fig tree. After the principles of the holy and divine laws of their forefathers.

9. All nations of the earth in these modern days are seeking peace, but there is but one true and divine way that peace may be obtained in these days and it is through Love, Truth, Peace, Freedom and Justice being taught universally to all nations, in all lands.

The End of Time And The Fulfilling of The Prophecies

1. The last Prophet in these days is Noble Drew Ali, who was prepared divinely in due time by Allah to redeem men from their sinful ways; and to warn them of the great wrath which is sure to come upon the earth.

2. John the Baptist was the forerunner of Jesus in those days, to warn and stir up the nation and prepare them to receive the divine Creed which was to be taught by Jesus.

3. In these modern days there came a forerunner, who was divinely prepared by the great God-Allah and his name is Marcus Garvey, who did teach and warn the nations of the earth to prepare to meet the coming Prophet; who was to bring the true and divine Creed of Islam, and his name is Noble Drew Ali; who was prepared and sent to this Earth by Allah, to teach the old time religion and the everlasting gospel to the sons of men. That every nation shall and must worship under their own vine and fig tree and return to their own and be one with their Father God-Allah.

4. The Moorish Science Temple of America is a lawfully chartered and incorporated organization. Any subordinate Temple that desires to receive a charter, the prophet has them to issue to every state throughout the United States, etc.

5. That the world may hear and know the truth, that among the descendents of Africa there is still much wisdom to be learned in these days for the redemption of the sons of men under Love, Truth, Peace, Freedom and Justice.

6. We, as a clean and pure nation descended from the inhabitants of Africa, do not desire to amalgamate or marry into the families of the pale skin nations of Europe. Neither serve the gods of their religion, because our forefathers are the true and divine founders of the first religious Creed, for the redemption and salvation of mankind on earth.

7. Therefore we are returning the church and Christianity back to the European Nations, as it was prepared by their forefathers for their earthly salvation.

8. While we, the Moorish Americans are returning to Islam, which was founded by our forefathers for our earthly and divine salvation.

9. The Covenant of the great God-Allah: "Honor thy father and thy mother that thy days may be longer upon the earth land, which the Lord thy God, Allah hath given thee"!

10. Come all ye Asiatics of America and hear the truth about your nationality and birthrights, because you are not Negroes. Learn of your forefathers ancient and divine Creed. That you will learn to love instead of hate.

Legal Exemption From Slavery

Expatriation

On July 27, 1868, One Day before the Fourteenth (14th) Amendment took effect, an "Act" of Congress was passed. This act was 15 United States Statute At Large, known as the Expatriation Statute. Though this statute is no longer included in the United States Code, it has not been repealed and is still in effect. This statute is extremely important because it is the public municipal law the individual can use for private purposes to remove him/her self from the private trust law operating in the public sector. That is, a private individual, who has found himself or herself bound by private law that is being used in the public sector to promote public policies of compelled performances which he did not have a choice in, can access the public positive statue law to move back under the liberty and protection of the Republic (Constitutional Form of Government=National Government) and its separation of powers.

The preamble of 15 United States Statute at Large is unique in that Congress laid the legal discussion to rest before the statute took effect to assure it would not be tampered with legally in any way. It stands as written and is there for the citizens to use as public law for the private purpose of moving themselves from one political or territorial jurisdiction to another. This means there is a way out at any time of any United States government policy or law, including those of its political subdivisions, that is based on private law. Whenever you find yourself bound by any compelled performance you had no choice in, you are operating in the jurisdiction of the United States government and its political subdivisions, where there is no Republican form of government and its separation of powers. By applying public laws for your private benefit you can break that dictatorial jurisdiction any time you choose.

The insidiousness of the 14th Amendment is that even though it is private contract law of a trust, it is not a bilateral contract where both parties signed the document after a meeting of the minds. The 14th Amendment is quasi contractual. That is, it is not a true contract as recognized in the general common-law. Rather it is called an adhesion or unilateral contract where only one party binds himself. In this case a person agrees to the private trust law merely by his silence. If a person does not speak up to let his choice be known, the trust will assume he or she is a part of and beneficiary of it.

They will assume that you have gifted your life to the trust for the benefits they have to offer.

Under the 14th amendment the citizen, who does not make his choice known for or against the trust relationship, is assumed to be a beneficiary because he has not stated otherwise.

As a beneficiary, you are an outlaw (undesirable= stateless person) as far as the Constitution is concerned. You are operating outside of the Constitution. While operating outside the Constitution you only have relative rights under the Bill of Rights and the Constitution, because private contract law takes priority over constitutional law.

After you have made the transition from under the 14th amendment as a statutory citizen to transform yourself into a Constitution citizen (common-law), you can then invoke the Guarantee Clause of the United States Constitution Article 4. Section 4. Clause 1, under which the federal government ensures for the states both a "Republican form of government" and "protection from invasion or internal insurrection".

15 United States Statutes at Large, CH. 249-250, PPS 223-224, Section 1, R.S. 1999 Title 8 U. S. C. Section 1481.

See attached document (one original copy of the 40th Congress Expatriation Statute)...

FOURTIETH CONGRESS. SESS II., Ch. 249, 250. 1868.

CHAP. CCXLIX – An Act concerning the Rights of American Citizens in foreign States.

July 27, 1868.

WHEREAS the right of expatriation is a natural and inherent right of all people, indispensable to the enjoyment of the rights of life, liberty, and the pursuit of happiness; and whereas in the recognition of this principle this government has freely received emigrants from all nations, and invested them with the rights of citizenship; and whereas it is claimed that such American citizens, with their descendents, are subjects of foreign states, owing allegiance to the governments thereof; and whereas it is necessary to the maintenance of public peace that this claim of foreign allegiance should be promptly and finally disavowed: Therefore,

Rights of American citizens in foreign states. **Preamble.**

Right of expatriation declared.

Be it enacted by the Senate and House of Representatives of the United States of America in Congress assembled, That any declaration, instruction, opinion, order, or decision of any officers of this government which denies, restricts, impairs, or questions the right of expatriation, is hereby declared inconsistent with the fundamental principles of this government.

Protection to naturalized citizens in foreign states.

Sec. 2. And be it further enacted, That all naturalized citizens of the United States, while in foreign states, shall be entitled to, and shall receive from this government, the same protection of persons and property that is accorded to native-born citizens in like situations and circumstances.

Release of citizens imprisoned by foreign governments to be demanded

Sec.3. And be it further enacted, That whenever it shall be made known to the President that any citizen of the United States has been unjustly deprived of his liberty by or under the authority of any foreign government, it shall be the duty of the President forthwith to demand of that government the reasons for such imprisonment, and if it appears to be wrongful and in violation of the rights of American citizenship, the President shall forthwith demand the release of such citizen, and if the release so demanded is unreasonably delayed or refused, it shall be the duty of the President to use such means, not amounting to acts of war, as he may think necessary and proper to obtain or effectuate such release and all the facts and proceedings relative thereto shall as soon as practicable be communicated by the President to Congress.

Facts to be communicated to Congress.

APPROVED, July 27, 1868.

"Proclamation of Nationality"

Sovereignty

"Declaration of Free National Name"

The Undersigned, A Member of the Moorish Perpetual Union, do declare pursuant to The Divine Constitution And Bylaws: Act 6 (Nationality Act) of the Moorish Science Temple of America and Amendment I (Sovereign Moorish Nationals) of the Moorish Great Seal Zodiac Constitution, enacted pursuant to Articles II, IV, & VI of the Zodiac Constitution, That I Am A Free Master Builder-Moorish-American by inheritance. Let the record reflect that I proclaim and maintain my Moorish Sovereign Status, which is my Natural Born Birthright, In Propria Persona, Sui Juris; as a Moorish-American/Moorish-National confirmed herein, hereafter and forever Moor. Furthermore, let the record reflect that an original copy of the undersigned Titus Connally-Bey's Natal Chart (Destiny Record), is listed herein and is free of all corporate and commercial encumbrances. Therefore, the undersigned invokes his inherited birth right Of Jus Soli (The Right of the Soil) as the Great I Am. Pursuant to the Nationality Act of the Moorish Science Temple of America Act-6; "With us all members must proclaim their nationality and we are teaching our people their nationality and their Divine Creed that they may know that they are a part and a partial of this said government. And know that they are not Negroes, Color Folks, Black People, or Ethiopians, because these names were given to slaves by slave holders in 1779 and lasted until 1865 during the time of slavery, but this is a new era of time now, and all men now must proclaim their free national name to be recognized by the government in which they live and the nations of the earth". The undersigned therefore invokes the Preamble of Article 15, Section 1 and 2 of the Universal Declaration of Human Rights; Section 1. "Everyone has a right to a nationality". Section 2. "No one shall be arbitrarily deprived of his nationality". Let the record reflect, that a Public Notice of Proclamation Must and will be given.

I SO EXERCISE, AFFIRM, CERTIFY AND INVOKE: _____

THIS_____, DAY OF_____20___A.D. Titus K. Connally-Bey

Seal of Authenticity

MATTHEW 21:42, 43, 44